YOU CAN
HELP

YOU CAN HELP

A Guide for Family & Friends
of Survivors of Sexual Abuse and Assault

Plus:
19 SURVIVORS
SHARE STORIES
OF RECOVERY

REBECCA STREET

For the millions of innocent people
who have suffered the shame and pain
of sexual abuse and assault, and for those
who have lovingly accompanied them
on their journey to healing.

Dear Reader,

It is my hope—and the hope of the nineteen survivors who have contributed to this book—that we have transformed the pain and loss in our own lives into something redemptive so that others will suffer less. If you have a family member or friend who is the victim of sexual abuse or assault, take heart for you are in a unique position to ease that person's pain. May the insights and suggestions offered on these pages help you as you seek to help the one you love. And if you are a survivor, perhaps giving this little book to a friend or family member will assist you in receiving the understanding you long for and deserve.

— R.S.

INTRODUCTION

Millions of Americans experience sexual trauma. One in four females and one in six males are sexually abused before the age of eighteen.[1,2] At least ten percent of people who were sexually abused in childhood will have periods of complete amnesia for their abuse, followed by experiences of delayed recall.[3] In addition, every 107 seconds, another American is sexually assaulted. Each year, there are about 293,000 sexual assaults. Sixty-eight percent of those assaults will go unreported.[4] Nearly one-third (31%) of all rape victims develop PTSD sometime during their lifetime.[5,6] And children are three times as likely to be victims of rape than adults.[7]

The statistics are staggering. And yet, because sexual abuse and assault top the list of taboos in our society, there is a pervasive secrecy that keeps millions of victims in the shadows. Survivors are discouraged not only from speaking about the crimes themselves, but from even speaking about the emotional and psychological ramifications. Unfortunately, this stigma further exacerbates the deep and persistent shame they already carry as a result of the wounds inflicted upon them. Somehow, we must all learn to wear our scars proudly. But if the tragic events of our lives are regarded as dirty secrets that must be kept at all costs, how is that possible?

All survivors need advocates. They need to tell their stories and they need loved ones to participate in the healing process. Recovery does not occur in a vacuum. However, for a myriad of complicated reasons, too often those in the best position to help—the family and friends of the victim—feel the least prepared to do so. Accordingly, their default position ends up being silence, not because of callousness, but because of feelings of powerlessness. Any survivor will tell you, silence is the biggest obstacle to recovery.

The exception to this widespread secrecy is whenever a sexual abuse scandal grabs the media's attention. Then, there is public recognition that sexual crimes are in fact a terrible scourge in our society and that the victims of these crimes deserve compassion. I know from experience that this collective acknowledgment can be somewhat reassuring, but soon the issue fades away as other scandals surface, and in terms of one-on-one interactions, nothing has changed.

Surely the question that begs asking on behalf of all these injured ones is: what can we do to help? For the vast majority of victims, the first response is to seek support from a licensed and knowledgeable therapist and/or receive crisis intervention. After all, the healing of trauma is far too complex a subject to be left solely in the hands of lay people. However, professional help is only part of the equation. And in terms of what friends and family can do, it seems reasonable that the very ones who have had their lives forever changed by sexual trauma—people like myself and the other survivors in this book—may have the best answers.

What many folks unfamiliar with emotional trauma do not understand is that an injury to the spirit can be as devastating as a physical injury to the body. Numerous survivors of sexual abuse and assault quite justifiably feel that their spirits have been confined to wheelchairs and, as a result, they are cut off from the possibilities of a healthy and full life. I have felt this way. However, like many victims of both emotional and physical injuries, I have discovered a resiliency in the human spirit that defies predictions.

You Can Help is divided into two parts. In Part One I share my own story of recovery and provide numerous insights and information from professionals as well as useful statistics. While my personal history serves as a backdrop, the purpose of these ten chapters is to share the experiential and learned knowledge I have accrued on my own path to healing. Covering a wide range of issues, each chapter is designed to inform and assist the reader in the difficult task of helping a loved one recover from sexual trauma. However, this book would be incomplete without Part Two.

Because there are many types of sexual abuse and assault, Part Two serves to broaden the discussion and bring light to a wide variety of survivor experiences and the complexities surrounding those experiences. In researching this part of the book, I was frankly unprepared for the overwhelming response from victims of every sexual crime imaginable, and I wish I could tell each story. Especially important to me was the fact that these courageous people wanted to participate so that friends and family would be given tools for helping, many saying things like "My family are good people, but they didn't know what to do." All nineteen participants in Part Two share what was most helpful and hurtful in their recovery process. Their stories, learned wisdom, and advice are invaluable. My own life has been immeasurably enriched by their contributions and I know yours will be as well.

Fans of mythology may be familiar with the legend of Parsifal that speaks directly to the central premise of this book. Part of the lore surrounding King Arthur and the

Roundtable is a story of the Grail King who has been mortally wounded and his kingdom turned into a wasteland. The only way this evil spell can be broken is by a true act of kindness motivated by love. It is the knight Parsifal whose generous heart leads him to break the enchantment, yet his kind act is surprisingly no more than a simple question. When he sees the wounded king, he is moved with compassion and gently asks, "What ails thee, my lord?" Immediately, the king and kingdom are healed. The lesson is, of course, that by recognizing, acknowledging, and affirming another's suffering, healing can miraculously take place. Interestingly enough, like many of us, Parsifal had an earlier opportunity to demonstrate this kindness, but he felt it was not "knightly" to ask questions. And so only years later, when he followed his heart, was he able to save both the king and the kingdom.

Surely, many of us wish to be like Parsifal. We want to ease the suffering of another, and yet often we simply do not know how. My dear friend Anne is a case in point. Generally a model of supreme composure, Anne came to see me one afternoon stoically fighting back tears because her precious daughter had revealed that she had been raped as a child by a cousin. Now at age twenty-four, she was finally confronting this devastation. Anne felt powerless to help and she also blamed herself for not realizing something was wrong at the time. But according to the Department of Justice, "Not all sexually abused children exhibit symptoms—some estimate that up to 40% of sexually abused children are asymptomatic."[8] At any rate, Anne was determined to give full maternal support, and knowing of my history, she arrived at my home armed with pen and paper in search of answers. I was grateful to be asked and proceeded to share with her my experiences as an incest survivor, citing those who have assisted me in the arduous task of overcoming my own trauma. It is Anne's poignant visit that motivated the writing of this book. I believe Anne represents huge numbers of people who are extremely well-intentioned but are just lacking in tools.

The fear, pain, and confusion you may feel over your loved one's trauma can be so overwhelming that it beckons avoidance, and so I wish to thank you for picking up this book. It is an act of empathy on your part and indicates a generous willingness to help that person. The good news is that statistics have proven again and again that social support plays a truly significant role in recovery. So let us begin to explore ways in which we can open our hearts and be of use. It is unlikely that the outcome will be as dramatic as in the legend of Parsifal, but make no mistake about it, healing is possible, and you can help.

PART ONE:
A PATH TO
HEALING

chapter one
MY TRAUMA: A BRIEF HISTORY

The details of my case have in common with all victims of sexual trauma the fact that they are horrific. Those of us who have been sexually victimized understand as few others do the pain and humiliation that result. And while my circumstances may be more extreme than some, I also had much more help than many in overcoming my injuries. It is also true that there are countless victims of far worse crimes. And so, it is in the context of both of theses realities that I share the following.

I grew up in the suburbs of Washington, DC, the fourth of five children and the only girl in a beautiful, all-American family. My father, who was the perpetrator, held a high-level job in the C.I.A. My mother was a lovely woman whose tragic flaws were self-absorption and living during a period in history when there were few options available for people in her position. She was no match for her alcoholic husband, who was at times emotionally and physically violent to her, and I have come to accept that protecting me would have resulted in consequences she was incapable of handling. My father molested me from the time I was a toddler and began raping me when I was nine. The abuse, which he labeled my "punishment," continued until I went to college. The smallest infractions—being late to dinner, arguing with one of my brothers—resulted in his violations. He also sexually abused members of my extended family, as well as people outside our family.

Like many victims of severe trauma, I suffered from a dissociative disorder. Because this is an area of confusion for some and a hot button issue for others, I have devoted quite a bit of space to it in Chapter Eleven. For now, suffice it to say that though my memories were repressed as a means of survival, symptoms of abuse—violent nightmares, hyper-vigilance, low self-esteem, excessive fear and anxiety—abounded.

Afraid that there was something deeply and inherently wrong with me for which I was somehow to blame, I fought to hide my shame and brokenness by tenaciously overcompensating. I still do. I was Sweetheart Queen in high school and on the Homecoming Court in college and proceeded to go through life projecting an image in public that was far removed from my emotional reality.

In 1989, as the mother of two children and a series regular on a daytime television show, I was finally strong enough to integrate the reality of my past. There are few things of which I am certain, but one is that no matter how unwanted the truth may be, it is the only path to wholeness. Though the memories were excruciating, this knowledge opened the gate to my eventual healing. I wish I could say that suddenly I became better, but my recovery was a slow and painful process.

My deepest regret is that there were times when my brokenness cost my children dearly. Even so, and despite my many mistakes, I have worked very hard to be the mother I never had. Indeed, in my relationships with my son and daughter, I have experienced enormous redemption because I was able to change history.

To be honest, I suspect I will always be, to an ever-lessening extent, overcoming the effects of my father's abuse. Nevertheless, I own my life now. It is authentic and joyful, replete with opportunities for continued growth, pride, clarity, and forgiveness. This is a miracle, and it did not happen in a vacuum.

Joseph Campbell said, "The purpose of the journey is compassion." We who have experienced deep suffering are given a unique though certainly unwelcome chance to know the reality of those words in ways far greater than our more fortunate brothers and sisters. Equally true is that this same suffering provides limitless opportunities for compassion to those who witness it. Though it is undeniably difficult, participating in the healing of a loved one is among the dearest gifts life offers.

If you want others to be happy, practice compassion.
If you want to be happy, practice compassion.
— THE DALAI LAMA

PRACTICAL TIPS

1. Do not compare one person's history with another's. You will always be able to find someone with more or less trauma than your loved one. It does not matter.

2. Obvious as this may seem, it is sadly often forgotten: it is not the victim's fault that she or he was abused or

sexually assaulted. It is essential for the one helping to be unequivocally clear about this. It can also be helpful to periodically remind the victim of this crucial fact since many survivors blame themselves.

3. Within the Jewish community, Holocaust survivors have been compassionately and consistently asked to communicate their experiences. Encouraging someone you love to verbally share or write his or her story and then relate it to you is an incredibly loving and affirming gesture.

4. Always believe your loved one and allow her or him the dignity of being innocent unless proven guilty. No one wishes more than the victim that what happened had not happened.

5. None of us can ever know the degree of suffering someone else may bear, but we can choose to bear some of that suffering. Do not only ask, "What can I do?" as it is a question some people may have difficulty answering. Take action regardless and do things that reflect your love and concern while always respecting the survivor's choices and right to confidentiality.

chapter two
PERMISSION TO TALK

The most important message contained in this book is that the shame the victim experiences is increased when she or he is not permitted to talk about the trauma. For this reason, the working title for my book was initially, *It Hurts More If You Don't Talk About It*. I think that is why so many survivors, especially in the early stages of recovery, speak inappropriately about the abuse, sometimes even telling people they have just met. The very act of speaking is a powerful effort to heal. Regrettably, a stranger can only hear the words; he or she cannot transform them the way a loved one could. As noted in the introduction, sexual trauma—particularly incest—is not only a taboo, it is at the top of the list. The synonyms for "taboo" in themselves imply an imposition for silence: *forbidden, unmentionable, unthinkable, banned, outlawed, prohibited*. In fact, it is generally considered bad form to discuss any trauma, not just that which is sexual, so that the person who suffered the trauma not only must endure the painful effects, but is often unintentionally disgraced for wanting to receive needed comfort and understanding.

If in their intimate relationships victims are made actively or passively to be silent, loneliness and humiliation will increase.

And therefore, when the tabooed information is spoken about, it may become a torrent of anger, bitterness, and recrimination instead of a healing dialogue. However, if the survivor feels understood and supported in the first place and is compassionately encouraged to incorporate his or her trauma into the relationship, there very likely will not be the messiness of a broken dam. The deep pain and undeserved feelings of shame that accompany sexual trauma cannot go unaddressed. Such feelings will be expressed in symptoms. Pretending "it didn't happen" may work for the observer, but it is not an option for the victim.

Think about children who are unloved and ignored and keep trying to get the attention they long for. People who have been sexually traumatized at any stage in life have had the most vulnerable part of them harmed. That harm demands acknowledgment. It is no wonder, then, that we have seen victims of sexual abuse receive settlements of literally millions of dollars. The damage is beyond remuneration.

There may be concerns that if trauma survivors are encouraged to openly share their struggles, Pandora's box will be unlocked and an endless outpouring will result. *Best to nip it in the bud for it's not healthy to dwell on such things.* Ironically, the opposite generally happens. When we are allowed to be open about how we have been affected, a huge weight is lifted, and, although the need to talk about it does not disappear, it most assuredly lessens.

In her excellent landmark book on child sexual abuse and other traumas entitled *Trauma and Recovery*, Dr. Judith Herman writes, "When the truth is finally recognized, survivors can begin their recovery. But far too often secrecy prevails, and the story of the traumatic event surfaces not as a verbal narrative but as a symptom."[9] Indeed, every expert I have ever read agrees that secrecy is the enemy of recovery. Dr. Dan

Gottlieb, the radio host of *Voices in the Family* and columnist for *The Philadelphia Inquirer*, said, "Trauma does more than steal a piece of our lives. It also steals our identity...Almost anyone who has experienced trauma will tell you they felt alienated and alone. That's why when we are traumatized, we need to tell our story—frequently, to whomever will listen. This process is our mind's way of trying to understand what happened and to search for care and nurture."[10]

For men, the burden of secrecy can be even greater. Dr. Julia M. Whealin, in her article "Men and Sexual Trauma," points out, "There is a bias in our culture against viewing the sexual assault of boys and men as prevalent and abusive. Because of this bias, there is a belief that boys and men do not experience abuse and do not suffer from the same negative impact that girls and women do. However, research shows that...boys and men can suffer profoundly from the experience...and often suffer from a sense of being different, which can make it more difficult for men to seek help."[11] The eight brave men who generously share their stories in Part Two will help you gain a greater understanding of the devastation suffered by countless boys and men. For a fuller exploration of the subject, I recommend two wonderful resources: the book *Victims No Longer: The Classic Guide for Men Recovering from Sexual Child Abuse* by Mike Lew and the website 1in6.org. Both address the painful and complicated issues surrounding the abuse of boys and also provide information for those who wish to help.

It is of course true that therapy and group work, including twelve step programs, offer opportunities for honest dialogue. However, that is not a replacement for the acceptance and understanding of family and close friends. Indeed, my therapist consistently told me that keeping secrets would exacerbate my shame and handicap my ability to heal. And so I began a process of disclosure that initially seemed impossible.

I am incredibly grateful to a handful of people who have not only given me permission over the years to talk about the incest whenever I have needed, but have actually pushed me to do so. I have been able to share the frightening nightmares, the irrational fears of being raped, and perhaps worst of all, the sense of dirtiness I have carried for what was done to my young body. By revealing these secrets and receiving love despite those revelations, I began to fathom that at my core I was a worthy human being. One friend actually convinced me that by sharing my story I was doing her a favor rather than the other way around, insisting that her life was immeasurably enriched by her participation in my healing. What an amazing gift.

The paradox is that those in the strongest position to help often never do. I am referring to family members now. Most people share a longing to be understood by their families, but this need is heightened for trauma survivors. When those who are supposed to know and love us best do not acknowledge our pain and loss, the profound sense of personal alienation caused by the trauma is exacerbated, and unfortunately, the indescribable shame that is part of the carnage of sexual victimization is deepened. Truly, I believe such behavior is generally the result of feelings of helplessness, misplaced responsibility (survivor's guilt), or both, rather than a lack of sympathy. And so I trust that as these well intentioned people come to understand the implications of their actions, they will wish to find appropriate ways of helping those dear ones in their lives, no matter how challenging the task.

We are healed of a suffering only by expressing it to the full.
— MARCEL PROUST

PRACTICAL TIPS

1. Give your loved one emotional permission to talk about the trauma. You can begin by creating a supportive environment where she or he feels understood and accepted.

2. It is important to be honest with yourself. Hearing about sexual crimes is very hard for most people, so it is normal and completely understandable in these circumstances to feel discomfort and sadness. However, such feelings need not prevent you from acting in a constructive manner.

3. If you don't know what to say, say things like:
   - *I'm so sorry for what happened to you.*
   - *You don't ever have to feel ashamed with me. I'm on your side.*
   - *I'm really proud of you.* (I believe these are among the most healing words anyone can hear. They still bring tears to me.)
   - *I want to help. Please tell me what I can do.*
   - *I love you and respect how hard you are trying to create a good life for yourself.*

- I know I haven't asked you to share what happened, but that was because I felt so helpless. I'm ready to listen now.

You will find many other examples of encouraging things to say in Part Two.

4. If it is too hard to broach the subject verbally, write a letter similar to this one to your loved one. Then make a date to discuss the letter.

Dear _____ ,

I realize that the trauma you experienced changed your life forever. I want you to know I love you and I am so sorry for all the pain you have endured. The problem is, I'm not very good at this and that is why I have been afraid to talk about it. That is also why I sometimes may seem cold or indifferent. However, I have come to understand that silence only makes things worse, and so I am ready to open my heart. Will you help me? I know it's difficult, but I would be honored if you were to share your feelings with me. Though I have never gone through the trauma you have, I can learn from you and become a better person by sharing in your pain.

5. Remember that though you are powerless to change the event, you are not powerless to participate in the healing. Even if your loved one chooses to talk to someone other than you about the trauma, try not to take it personally and be one hundred percent assured that your openness and generosity of heart are making a difference.

chapter three
A COMPASSIONATE LENS

I will use myself as a prime example of what I am hoping to illustrate. I took a screenwriting class at UCLA. I was working on a semi-autobiographical comedy about a middle-aged actress trying to make it in Hollywood. One of the class assignments was to write a biography for the lead character. Easy for me—I simply and truthfully wrote my own history (with the name changed, of course, and in the guise that it was all fiction). The professor, a successful screenwriter, critiqued the bio and told me it was totally unrealistic. He said that (a) anyone who had experienced the kind of extended abuse that "Miranda" had suffered would be in a mental institution, and (b) that the character appeared to be a total ditz—married first to an ivory tower lawyer, then to a gay man, and then to a lying crack addict. He kindly suggested I rewrite it and make the protagonist believable. I never told him that every word was true and that the mental institution candidate/ditz was none other than the bright-eyed woman in front of him. He was a good teacher, and I understand his position, for I too would be suspicious if I heard about someone like me.

So, what is the point? Well, there are significant people

in my life who view my three marriages as proof of personal irresponsibility and flakiness, stemming from some unattended weakness of character. In fact, one response was: "You can't keep hurting the family like this." To be clear, I am an adult and I am accountable for my own behavior. However, such assessments are strong on judgment and weak on compassion and have been quite hurtful to me, even though I am sure that was not the intent. Each of my divorces was more heartbreaking than the prior one. I am profoundly saddened that my actions hurt my children and mortified that my life reads like a bad movie of the week. After all, I take very seriously my commitments; I work hard, I go to church on Sundays, I pay my bills on time, and I try my best to live with integrity. Not to mention that I have spent over $75,000 of my hard-earned money on therapy, trying to heal my life. And yet, I have royally screwed up. How could I have been so foolish? I have asked that question with shame and regret repeatedly.

Fortunately, since I have finally learned to be my own advocate, the answer is not too complicated. Viewed through a lens of compassion, I am someone who was afraid to sleep alone at night, whose personal shame has deeply impacted my perception of myself and others, and for whom relationships with men may always be distorted. I remember telling a pastor: "Both _____ and I have terrible histories; he's a recovering crack addict and I'm an incest survivor." I never saw a difference. I never felt that someone like me had the right to judge anyone else. And of course at the time—like most of us—I had what I believed were sound reasons for entering into all three marriages. My first marriage to the father of my children lasted fifteen years, and, though it was problematic from the start, we raised two wonderful children. I met the gay man at church. He is a doctor of psychology, and we were on an AIDS council together. And my third and most disastrous marriage, which was annulled on the basis of fraud, was to someone I believed to be the kindest person I had ever met.

The truth is relationships carried the false promise of ending my pain and making me feel safe. I wanted so badly to feel loved that I just kept trying. In addition to my three marriages, I was engaged five other times. Trust is a major issue for survivors. Many trust too little or not at all; others, particularly those who struggle with dissociation, trust too much. I fall into the latter category. Regardless of the ways we act out, victims will naturally search for release from the suffering caused by abuse or assault and many will be drawn to a myriad of unhealthy behaviors that offer even temporary liberation.

It follows then that for many survivors, "drug and alcohol consumption are likely to be companions in the victim's attempt to gain relief," and compared to non-victims of crimes, rape victims are 13.4 times more likely to have major alcohol problems and twenty-six times more likely to have drug abuse problems.[12] Also alarming is a National Institute of Justice study which found "that childhood abuse increased the odds of future delinquency and adult criminality overall by 29 percent."[13] These upsetting statistics are a powerful counter to the widespread tendency in our culture to minimize the impact of sexual trauma on the victim.

Again, viewing your loved one and his or her actions through a lens of compassion does not mean there should be an absence of accountability. In an interview entitled, "Reflections on Compassion and Social Healing," the award-winning Dr. Judith Thompson concludes, "From within the healing paradigm, we look for the root causes...Clearly, you do have to have norms and laws and...name wrong behavior when you see it. But a compassionate person looks beyond the wrongdoing into where the roots of it are." Dr. Thompson also reminds us, "Compassion can transform a situation of entrenched enmity, hopelessness, or despair and open us to new perspectives of what's possible."[14]

Showing compassion and giving the benefit of the doubt to loved ones are always good ideas, but with survivors of trauma, such generosity can literally be life changing. Sadly, the survivor often begins the day feeling damaged, and her or his mistakes simply act to reinforce that fear. When a family member or friend is sympathetic rather than disapproving, it can go a long way in removing the stigma. Of course, we are likely to fall more than others. That is a given, not an excuse.

If you judge people, you have no time to love them.
— MOTHER TERESA OF CALCUTTA

PRACTICAL TIPS

1. Always choose understanding over judgment. A person in pain will be far more open to sharing mistakes as well as receiving guidance when you respond with love rather than condemnation. And remember, many of the mistakes your loved one makes could well be directly related to the trauma.

2. Do not put your loved one in the terrible position of having to pretend to be okay so that you feel better. If you yourself are struggling with how to deal with the issue (which is understandable), you may find short term counseling helpful. It will provide you with support and give you tools for handling the situation.

3. As is clearly illustrated by the other survivors in this book, it is important to realize that each person deals with trauma differently. I sought comfort in relationships. Someone else may use drugs or alcohol, be a cutter, have an eating disorder, lie, rage, be promiscuous, isolate, escape into fantasy, etc. At the same time, there are some survivors who internalize their pain and display no obvious symptoms whatsoever.

4. Try to be proactive. If the trauma survivor is searching for relief in unhealthy ways, don't be afraid to lovingly show your concern. Writing notes of encouragement is a wonderful way to do this. Suggesting that he or she get professional help is important. If the person cannot afford therapy, offering financial help—at least initially—is a wise investment.

5. Though your motives may be good, definitely avoid saying things like:
- But it happened so long ago.
- Isn't it time for you to put that behind you and get on with your life?
- So and so had a much worse thing happen and they're doing okay.

- *Dwelling on it doesn't help.*

And do not ask irrelevant question about circumstances such as clothing worn or alcohol consumed or the timeline of the abuse or assault. Such questions imply culpability and/or doubt and are very hurtful. No one is to blame here except the perpetrator.

chapter four
THE POWER OF PRAISE

The subject of praise and the widespread tendency to withhold it is a topic of puzzling interest to me. Recently, my children and I reflected together on this phenomenon, which seems to exist in the classroom, the workplace, and the home. Surely it is an undisputed fact that we human beings do better when we receive praise. Besides the fact that praise produces good results, isn't it fun to give as well? Enough pondering. This is a philosophical conundrum that cannot be solved by the likes of me. I simply wish to say that I realize trauma survivors have not been singled out and deprived of emotional boosts bestowed on the rest of the population.

Accepting that we are all probably denied the praise we crave and deserve then, I would like to make a case for the fact that, though it may bring pleasure to one person, it can be truly curative to another. When a person's self-esteem has been seriously impaired by trauma, praise is like an antibiotic; it can help get rid of the poison. If the scales in one's psyche are weighted heavily on the side of shame and self-loathing, which is exactly what sexual trauma does, praise adds weight to the side of wholeness and self-acceptance. In these instances, it is not a narcissistic luxury but a critically needed truth serum.

For those of you who know but are not intimate with a victim of trauma, do not underestimate the impact your display of approval may have upon that person. Aside from my wonderful younger brother Tom, the most "significant other" in my childhood was my fourth grade teacher at St. Martin's Elementary School. Sister Catherine William was immensely kind to me, and somehow I got the feeling she believed me to be the most special child in her class. (I would not be surprised to learn that many of the children believed the same to be true of themselves.) She always praised my penmanship, and to this day I am unduly proud of my skillful use of the Palmer method of handwriting. I have no way of knowing and therefore can only speculate that she was cognizant of my struggles with self-esteem, but at any rate, she selected me to be the star of our Christmas play. It would be many years before I could be on stage with any joy again. In fact, I was thirty before I built up the courage to take an acting class. It was Sister Catherine William's praise of me in that little Christmas play that gave me the sweetest of all memories I have from those difficult years. You teachers, who rarely see the results of your dedication, take heart.

Appearances, as we all know, can be misleading. Therefore, do not be deceived by your loved one's ability to act "normal," and do not assume that the exterior reflects the interior. (Remember Edwin Arlington Robinson's poignant poem "Richard Cory?") I have fought tenaciously to cover my neediness, knowing few things are perceived as being less attractive, and I have been rather successful at doing so. However, the amount of internal suffering I have experienced as a result of the incest and the lack of self-esteem it caused is incalculable.

After college, I lived in New York City for a year, and despite wonderful prospects, I spent hours secretly trying to devise a way to commit suicide that would seem like an accident, so as to spare my family. In fact, though I never spoke of it (except to therapists), thoughts of suicide plagued me for decades. As an actress, I was nearly forced to abandon the work I love and have been gifted to do because of crippling nervousness on auditions. I have experienced an embarrassing level of self-consciousness and anxiety in most social situations. Yet were you to meet me during those years, you would have been struck by my beauty and charm, while I would go home punitively recounting my every "blunder" and wishing I could be someone else—anyone else. I chronicle these things not to highlight my own woes for I know full well that I have suffered far less than many on this planet. I do so to give a glimpse into the private struggles of many trauma survivors and to alert you to the dichotomy of appearances and reality.

Praise can be difficult to accept for someone who cannot believe good things about herself or himself. And unfortunately, we humans generally not only attract but often choose people who mirror the image we hold of ourselves, causing a vicious cycle. Therefore your kind words may initially seem unwanted and unappreciated, but this will change.

Needless to say, praise should always be sincere and honest, or it will not mean anything. Each human being is a wonder, and there are attributes to be commended both on the inside and outside of us all. Had I only known my actual value, my experiences would have been very, very different. Praise is a way of helping your loved ones recognize and celebrate their uniqueness, thereby giving them a greater chance for a better life.

I can live for two months on a good compliment.

— MARK TWAIN

PRACTICAL TIPS

1. Write a list just for yourself, joyfully detailing the positive qualities your loved one possesses. You may be pleasantly surprised at what you discover. Perhaps breaking it into categories will help you be specific. For example:

- *virtues*
- *physical attributes*
- *skills and talents*
- *knowledge*

2. Make a point of regularly mentioning those things, especially when circumstances dictate their appropriateness. You can make a game out of being extra observant.

- *You were very nice to that salesgirl; I love how kind you are.*
- *You look absolutely beautiful in your new dress.*
- *What an amazing cook you are.*
- *You're incredibly knowledgeable about music; I learn so much from you.*
- *Your essay is terrific; you're really smart.*
- *I appreciate how hard you work.*
- *You'll be the most handsome man at the party.*

- Thank you for cleaning the house; you're such a thoughtful person.
- That drawing is wonderful; you're extremely talented.

3. Remember it is essential to be honest. Hollow praise will always backfire.

4. Even when someone fails or comes up short, encouragement can be used.
- You did your best and that's all I care about.
- Don't beat up on yourself; we all make mistakes.
- So you didn't get that job; you'll get the next one.
- I do silly things, too.

5. Watch as your praise has the effect of rain on a seedling and be sure to praise yourself for praising.

chapter five
NO EXCUSES (FOR THE INEXCUSABLE)

This is a short chapter because its essential purpose is to qualify and clarify the suggestions being offered throughout the pages of this book—a sort of timeout, if you will. Lest I have given the wrong impression, I want to acknowledge that I do not think trauma survivors deserve immunity from unacceptable behavior any more than anyone else. Though trauma may explain certain actions, it does not excuse the inexcusable. Nor do I advocate special treatment, which more often than not is an indicator of pity or fear rather than understanding.

In all our interactions, it is important that participants practice a modicum of kindness, dignity, and respect. This goal in no way precludes the normal and healthy expression of negative emotions, including anger. Clearly, anger is almost always an inevitable result of trauma and should not be squelched, as it is generally a part of the healing process. Nevertheless, tolerating abuse from one who has been abused is a terrible mistake and only perpetuates the cycle of sickness. Certainly, it is a great sadness that many who have been injured try to relieve their pain by injuring others.

It is impossible to predict the way anyone will respond to trauma. After all, there are an infinite number of variables that determine such responses. Why do people who are raised similarly or share comparable challenges and setbacks often react in such dramatically different ways? In relation to the protagonist in his bestseller, In Cold Blood, Truman Capote acknowledged the social parallels between himself and the infamous killer, Perry Smith. He said of their childhoods, "It's as if Perry and I grew up in the same house and he stood up and went out the back door while I went out the front." How does that happen? Indeed, I have been disturbed for as long as I can remember by the perplexing and often extreme disparity of human reactions to similar circumstances. Wouldn't it be wonderful if we could bottle and distribute courage, self-esteem, and morality? (And keep it out of the hands of pharmaceutical companies.)

Lastly, I wish to clearly state that the recommendations offered here are not directed toward those unfortunate victims who are acting out in overtly destructive or abusive ways. Their problems are beyond the scope of this book and should be addressed by professionals. Rather, my insights and the insights of the survivors in Part Two are intended for the many, many victims of trauma who are bravely and sincerely trying to heal their lives and for whom a helping hand may make all the difference.

God, grant me the serenity to accept the things I cannot change,
the courage to change the things I can,
and the wisdom to know the difference.

— REINHOLD NIEBUHR

PRACTICAL TIPS

1. Be as honoring to yourself as you are to the person who has experienced the trauma.

2. Be clear that no amount of trauma is a license for hateful behavior. You need not and should not tolerate disrespect from anyone. If you are having trouble setting boundaries, get psychological or spiritual counseling, or both. The principles laid out by Al-Anon are also useful in learning to set boundaries.

3. Remember that helping your loved one is not the same thing as enabling her or him. Giving money you know is going to be used for drugs, making excuses, or lying to cover up irresponsible behavior, etc. only hurts you and postpones the victim's recovery.

4. Seek professional and/or legal help for yourself if your loved one is physically abusive. By all means, remove yourself from any situation that is potentially dangerous.

5. Do not interfere where you are clearly not wanted. (Obviously, I am speaking of adult victims, not children.) Furthermore, do not assume it is your fault if someone consistently rejects your love and support. Ultimately, each of us is responsible for the life we create.

chapter six
PTSD AND THE LONG HAUL

If only we could all do our part and the whole bloody thing would be over, like a terrible dream from which we could awaken. Unfortunately, that is rarely the case. I spent over a decade working with a highly skilled clinical psychologist, determined to overcome my trauma. At the conclusion of our work, I reveled in the fact that I had experienced a healing greater than I had imagined possible and felt extremely optimistic about my future. It was deeply disturbing, therefore, when bouts of post-traumatic stress disorder (PTSD) and severe depression continued to intermittently disrupt my life.

Psychology Today defines post-traumatic stress disorder as "an anxiety disorder that may develop after exposure to a terrifying event or ordeal in which severe physical harm occurred or was threatened."[15]

There are many wonderful websites giving in-depth and documented information on PTSD. For its breadth and clarity, The U.S. Department of Veterans Affairs, National Center for PTSD is my favorite. Perhaps, the most obvious illustrations of PTSD have to do with soldiers returning from combat. Such stimuli as the sound of a helicopter or even a breaking dish can cause a person to relive the trauma suffered on the battlefield. The U.S. Department of Veterans Affairs states that thirty-one percent of Vietnam veterans have been victims of this disorder at some time in their lives.[16] It makes one wonder if there would be fewer homeless vets with placards asking for money had their trauma been acknowledged and addressed.

This website also discusses many other causes of PTSD besides combat. The most common are rape, molestation, physical attack, childhood neglect, physical abuse, and witnessing a violent act. And as stated in the introduction, nearly one-third of all rape victims develop rape-related PTSD some time during their lifetimes, and more than eleven percent still suffer from it.[17] Indeed, I found one of the more startling statistics to be that 7-8% of the population will have PTSD at some point in their lives.[18]

Many people are unfamiliar with PTSD and its effects. Therefore, it behooves us to take a close look at the behaviors and feelings associated with this disorder so that we can help those suffering from it. According to the *Medical Encyclopedia*, a service of the U.S. National Library of Medicine and the National Institute of Health, symptoms of PTSD fall into these three general categories:

1. Repeated "reliving" of the event, which disturbs day to-day activity
   - Recurrent distressing memories of the event
   - Recurrent dreams of the event
   - Flashback episodes, where the event seems to be recurring
   - Bodily reactions to situations that remind them of the traumatic event

2. Avoidance
   - Inability to remember important aspects of the trauma
   - Lack of interest in normal activities
   - Feelings of detachment
   - Sense of having no future
   - Emotional numbing or feeling as though they don't care about anything
   - Reduced expression of moods
   - Staying away from places, people, or objects that remind them of the event

3. Arousal
   - Irritability or outbursts of anger
   - Sleeping difficulties
   - Difficulty concentrating
   - Exaggerated response to things that startle them
   - Hyper-vigilance[20]

In addition to the type of PTSD that results from traumatic events of time-limited duration such as rape, Dr. Judith Herman of Harvard University (cited in Chapter Two) suggests that a new diagnosis called Complex PTSD is needed to describe the symptoms of long-term trauma. Though ninety-two percent of individuals with Complex PTSD also meet criteria for PTSD, there are additional symptoms worthy of review.[20] "Complex PTSD, also known as disorder of extreme stress, is found among individuals who have been exposed to prolonged traumatic circumstances, especially during childhood, such as childhood sexual abuse. Research shows that many brain and hormonal changes may occur as a result of early, prolonged trauma...Combined with a disruptive, abusive home environment, these brain and hormonal changes may contribute to severe behavioral difficulties such as eating disorders, impulsivity, aggression, inappropriate sexual behavior, alcohol or drug abuse, and other self-destructive actions, as well as emotional regulation (such as intense rage, depression, or panic) and mental difficulties (such as scattered thoughts, dissociation, and amnesia)."[21]

I have experienced many of the above symptoms in my road to recovery. For years, the most debilitating part of PTSD was always the haunting fear that I would never be okay. And yet, I am okay. As I get older and experience more and more healing, the incest has less impact on my life. Nightmares are few and far between. I used to have my sleep interrupted when I was alone and, in stark terror, would go around my home checking the windows, sure that someone would break in and harm me. And during the day, I would be completely overcome with panic when someone startled me. Those things no longer happen.

However, there are still times when PTSD rears its ugly head and unwanted memories unexpectedly pierce my heart anew, filling me with shame. And when that happens, the act of speaking and being validated remains an important component in lessening the pain. Ironically, even with all my understanding, my embarrassment can often force me to silence. Believe me, I am wearier than anyone with this whole ghastly business. But because I know that I am not to blame, I try to share my symptoms with a trusted friend or seek professional help, knowing such action will help me get better and shorten my pain.

I suspect it is our sense of helplessness and our own unique, personal struggles that make us so impatient. And yet, if symptoms remain, they remain. That in no way negates the fact that progress has been made or that the potential for a healthy life remains intact. We must value the integrity and dignity inherent in effort. Confucius said, "It does not matter how slowly you go so long as you do not stop."

The two most powerful warriors are patience and time.
— LEO TOLSTOY

PRACTICAL TIPS

1. Understanding the complexities of the healing process is very difficult; the other survivor stories will further assist you in this complicated task. Recovery is individual and dependent upon a myriad of variables.

2. Unfortunately, there are those who, through no fault of their own, never fully recover from the effects of trauma. Indeed, some people suffer from PTSD their entire lives. Do not inadvertently suggest that such people are responsible for the duration of their pain. On the other hand, there are many whose recovery time is relatively short, and, though the sting of the memories remains, their injuries cease to overtly impact their lives.

3. Offer an emotional and physical refuge for your loved one when he or she struggles with PTSD and other

effects of trauma. Give the person the same love and nurturance that you would if he or she was physically ill. And remember to strongly urge the survivor to get professional help if the situation is dire.

4. Humbly accept that unless you have experienced something first-hand, you can never truly comprehend what another person is going through. Therefore do not try to talk the victim out of his or her feelings.

5. Sticking it out through the long haul is very difficult, and feelings of impatience, weariness, and even anger may arise. However, the personal rewards for such faithfulness are significant, and the benefits of such loyalty to the survivor are incalculable. I suspect there is far more regret for not caring enough than for caring too much.

chapter seven
LISTENING

At first glance, this chapter may seem redundant with "Permission to Talk." Yet, encouraging someone to speak and actually hearing what he or she says are two vastly different skills. Webster defines the word "listen" as "to give attention with the ear." I propose an alternative definition: to give attention with the heart. In the beloved classic *The Little Prince*, Antoine de Saint-Exupery wrote, "It is only with the heart that one can see rightly; what is essential is invisible to the eye." Surely the same is true of listening. It is only with the heart that one can hear rightly.

When I was going through my memories, my older brother Jim was my guardian angel. Before I had the courage to tell my family, I called him and said I had something important I needed to talk about and that I couldn't do it on the phone. At the time, he lived in D.C. and I in L.A. Three days later, he was on an airplane. During our time together and for many months afterwards, he listened and listened and listened. Sometimes, his jaw would tighten and flex and his eyes would betray an unutterable sadness, but still he would listen. Of course, he also responded, for he wisely knew that without a response, there is no proof of having been heard. However, this successful businessman, who has spent his life finding answers, never presumed to have answers for my pain. Rather, he said things like, "I'm so sorry," "I wish I had known so I could have protected you," "I'm very proud of how strong you are," and "You mustn't give up; many people love you." Though some of what I shared had to disgust him, and the implications for him were profound since I was speaking of our father and not just my father, he never wavered. He, more than anyone, carried me across the bridge from despair to acceptance, and gave me hope during that wilderness journey. He did it by encouraging me to talk, compassionately listening, and believing in me. It could not have been easy for him.

The director of the Center for Loss and Life Transition and a member of the University of Colorado Medical school faculty, Dr. Alan Wolfelt says, "Helping begins with your capacity to be an active listener. Your physical presence and desire to listen without judgment are critical helping tools. Don't worry so much about what you will say. Just concentrate on listening to and empathizing with the words that are being shared with you."[22]

I know first hand that listening can be tough. When I am unable to truly listen, it is generally because I cannot accept what I am hearing. When something is said to me, which seems to imply that I have made a blunder, I do not hear the words; I hear an accusation. I am not listening. Were I actually listening, I would hear the other person's dilemma, disappointment, or despondency. There are also times when I hear pain from someone I love, and because I cannot bear when those I love suffer, rather than listening, I choose the easier task of reacting. Listening makes it too real, too unsolvable, which it often is. Since I pride myself on being a great problem solver, my children have had to remind me more than once that they have not come to me for answers but rather solely for the comfort inherent in sharing sorrows or struggles with someone who loves them.

In terms of trauma, there are rarely solutions, and certainly there are no simple solutions wrapped up in our favorite platitudes. Perhaps when we accept that unhappy fact, we can lay down the impossible burden of trying to make it all right. If we grasp that our gift is not to fix but to show empathy, our contribution can be astounding.

Pragmatically speaking, if your loved one makes a reference to the trauma, allow it; do not change the subject or make a judgment. If the person makes a negative observation about himself or herself or cracks a self-deprecating joke that shows a lack of self-esteem, simply counter it with something positive rather than punitive. Though it may seem obvious, I reiterate that it is insensitive to ignore someone's attempts to be heard by remaining silent. A response—even an imperfect one—is an essential component to the listening process. A kind response is a healing component.

Listening has transformative powers for the one being listened to and the listener. This I believe to be true for all of us in all circumstances, regardless of our own unique histories. Paradoxically, the benefits of lovingly listening are far greater than our fervent and generally futile attempts to repair a situation.

With the gift of listening comes the gift of healing.
— CATHERINE DE HUECK

PRACTICAL TIPS

1. Listening with your heart is not a complicated task. It only requires practice, and it is a skill that will benefit all areas of your life. Hearing is not listening. As Stravinsky wryly noted, "A duck hears also."

2. It is helpful to know that not everyone is expected to assume the burdensome role taken on by my brother Jim. I suspect few people have this ability. Nevertheless, even occasional efforts to share in your loved one's loss can have a wonderfully regenerative effect. And for those who are all in, Part Two offers further poignant examples of the ways people can fully participate in the recovery of their loved ones.

3. The best essay that I have ever read on the healing power of listening is in Dr. Rachel Naomi Remen's *Kitchen Table Wisdom* (specifically aimed for people living with cancer but with applications for all suffering people). You may wish to look at it.

4. When listening, it is essential that you verbally acknowledge what you have heard. The reply should mirror—that is, specifically address—the words spoken to you. In other words, if your loved one says, "I had a terrible nightmare last night," you could counter with something like: "I am so sorry that you suffer from nightmares. Would it help to talk about it?" (The mirroring is in the repetition of the word "nightmare.")

5. Again, remember it is not your job to fix it, and, even if you wanted to, you would not be able to do so. Therefore you need not worry about the perfect response. Simply and genuinely try to react with love and concern.

chapter eight
FUN

Given the preoccupation thus far with trauma and healing, I suspect anything remotely buoyant will come as a pleasant, if only partial, respite. Exactly the point. The observations presented in this book may be wearisome to contemplate for the reader, who can choose at any point to put the book down, but for trauma survivors these matters are daily fare. Diversions from such weightiness not only provide a much needed reprieve for the survivor, but when the diversions carry with them lightness and joy, they are immensely therapeutic.

Life must not be reduced to a problem that requires solving or a burden that we heroically shoulder. I am, as I admitted earlier, a hopeless problem solver, and I believe this to be true for many trauma survivors. After all, searching for solutions seductively holds out the promise of deliverance from the destruction born of abuse and other loss. And though understanding is crucial, trauma cannot be approached like a mathematical equation. We must find ways to navigate the world of mystery, to discover meaning in the moment, and most certainly, we must learn to have fun.

If trauma occurs when someone is a child, the likelihood is that the state we call childhood will be aborted and much that is fondly associated with childhood is lost. It is as if the victim suddenly and sadly grows up. If only such growing up ushered in an acquisition of wisdom; but no, it simply results in a loss of innocence and a conscious or subconscious knowledge of evil relegated for those who have lived longer. Children who have been abused at a young age rarely know afterwards what it feels like to be truly carefree. The ability to play with abandon is generally stolen from them. And so they must be re-educated.

Not surprising is the fact that "rape victims are 4.1 times more likely than non-crime victims to contemplate suicide."[23] Indeed, all trauma survivors, regardless of the time of their trauma, generally have to begin again the brave and formidable task of opening their hearts to the wonders of a universe that has the same potential for benevolence as it does for malevolence. How then does one go about reclaiming joy? There are endless volumes with spiritual answers to that question, but here we will simply look at uncomplicated actions that reaffirm the life process. We will venture forth into the world of play, seeking ways to have pure, unadulterated fun.

It is true that few things are more healing than laughter, so trauma survivors in particular need frequent doses of humor. My son gave me a DVD of *Waiting for Guffman* for my birthday some years ago. Maybe it is because I am an actress, but this delightful Christopher Guest film makes me laugh, almost to the point of tears, every time I watch it. What a wonderful tonic. Since survivors of trauma deal with a disproportionate degree of darkness, any opportunity to experience light is truly like glimpsing a rainbow. Happily, occasions for rainbow spotting abound, and, needless to say, making them available to those struggling ones we love is a worthy enterprise.

Norman Cousins, editor of *The Saturday Review* for over forty years and later a faculty member of the UCLA School of Medicine, provided evidence for the curative powers of laughter in his best selling book, *Anatomy of an Illness as Perceived by the Patient: Reflections on Healing and Regeneration*. In the 1960s, Cousins was afflicted with a life-threatening disease, during which time he followed a regimen that included daily doses of belly laughter. He reported laughing uncontrollably while watching old Marx Brothers movies and was convinced that his own laughter contributed significantly to his recovery. Cousins believed that "the life force may be the least understood force on earth" and that "human beings are not locked into fixed limitations."[24] If laughter can help cure the body, imagine what it can do for the spirit.

Many opportunities for fun are free, but for those that are not, if the person you love cannot afford such luxuries and you can, making these experiences available is a wise use of money. Survivors frequently have trouble indulging in frivolous distractions and often any form of self-pampering feels undeserved. I could always be generous with others but would not dare treat myself even to an issue of *Vogue*. After one of my divorces, a dear friend flew me to Maui so that I could spend a week of healing reflection on the beach. I mention this because it was a component in my own recovery, and I will always be grateful, but I am not proposing such grand gestures are necessary or expected. Giving a favorite CD, a bouquet of flowers, a dinner at a special restaurant—these are all wonderful overtures. And if finances are tight, do not worry; the best gifts are always gifts from the heart and not the wallet.

Playing is a skill most of us have forgotten and would do well to re-learn. Why not let trauma be redemptive, allowing it to provide motivation for such relearning? In twelve step programs, choosing fun in the midst of pain is called contrary action. If your loved one is not strong enough to take contrary action, you can provide it. Surely sharing fun with someone you love is the epitome of a win-win situation.

He deserves Paradise who makes his companions laugh.

— THE KORAN

PRACTICAL TIPS

1. Physical exercise is terrific. Some forms of exercise release serotonins, widely believed to affect emotional states. Suggest a jog, a hike, or a tennis match together. Less strenuous but lots of fun are bowling and miniature golf. I am a big proponent of silliness, and these latter two seem to lend themselves to a special type of playfulness.

2. A good movie is a fantastic escape, and of course a great comedy can be truly mood-altering. Also included in this category are live theater and stand-up comedy. (Some of my personal favorites are Steve Martin, Ellen DeGeneres, Louis C.K., Eddie Izard, and Richard Pryor.)

3. Being in nature provides a quieter but deeply satisfying contentment. Ann Frank, whose brief life is a symbol of triumph over adversity, said, "I firmly believe that nature brings solace in all troubles." Picnics in the park,

sitting under the stars, visiting the beach, watching a sunset—these are all activities sure to comfort and cheer.

4. Pets can supply comfort, company, and to many, are a great source of joy. Also, dogs often help survivors feel safer because of the barking that generally accompanies unexpected sounds. I joke that my relationship with my little dog Fulton is the best relationship with a male I've ever had.

5. Concerts are wonderful, but all music can create pleasure, and you do not have to go anywhere to enjoy it. Putting on an upbeat CD can change the mood in a room. And dancing—at home or out on the town—is an exercise in exuberance.

chapter nine
THE WHOLE PERSON

I am using the word "whole" here to mean the entire—not necessarily the intact—person. Each of us is a complex composite of a myriad of things. For example, I am a mother, a Christian, an actor, a writer, a sister, a friend, an incest survivor, and a social activist. I do not want to be defined by any one of these and certainly not to the exclusion of the others, for I am less than and more than all of them.

"Suffer us not to mock ourselves with falsehood," said T.S. Eliot in "The Wasteland." If something as major and life-changing as sexual trauma is not permitted to be a part of the composite of a person, it is a mockery to that person's humanity. I like Sly and the Family Stone's counter: "Thank you for letting me be myself." What could be sweeter?

A while back, I had dinner with a few women friends, and, because we are all middle-aged, single, and heterosexual, we naturally landed upon the subject of men. We discussed our past relationships as well as our prospective hopes. I spoke of a man I had been engaged to and who had been wonderful in his acceptance of me and my history. For many reasons, my gentleman friend and I were not a suitable match, but we had a lot of fun together, and he had a remarkable understanding of all the things that I have shared on these pages. Because of this, I experienced much healing during our four years together. At any rate, one of the women—a beautiful model and a gracious human being—suggested that were I to become involved with a man in the future, perhaps it would be better if I kept the incest a secret. I was stunned. The implication of such a remark is that I am a more desirable candidate without that information. Well, I know that! The rub is that I do not want to be with someone who is repelled or frightened by my history. The real truth is I do not want to be intimately involved with *anyone* who cannot accept with intelligence and compassion this aspect of who I am. My dinner companion certainly did not mean to hurt me, though she did. Essentially she highlighted what I already know: this part of me is perceived as shameful and makes many people feel queasy. However, it is who I am. It is not all of who I am, but it is still who I am. It does not make me unworthy, although that is not an easy conclusion to reach when it is so often treated in this fashion.

Though it is generally the case that the acknowledgement of trauma is omitted from interactions, sometimes the very opposite happens. Sometimes a survivor is seen exclusively as a victim, and this role becomes dominant in the relationship. This is equally injurious, for once again, it negates the whole person. Such labeling can be the result of either kindness or contempt, but regardless it will not assist in healing your loved one. Frequently, we have seen instances in our society when we decide what a person can or cannot contribute based on handicaps, and, without fail, we are shocked into realizing that our narrow perceptions are simply inaccurate.

Limited definitions are not always imposed by others. It is also a fact that many survivors choose to identify themselves primarily by the trauma they have suffered. This is especially true in the beginning and when the trauma and its effects on the victim are particularly profound or ignored. The darkness can prevent light from getting through, and all the other and varied qualities that are part of who the victim actually is become obfuscated. Again, the best salve for this condition is acceptance of the whole person. Generously responding to the wounded while celebrating the healthy and heroic qualities your loved one possesses will, I believe in time, allow the survivor to reflect back the whole person you determine to see.

For me, the desire to be whole, to allow my trauma to be gracefully woven into the colorful tapestry that is my life remains a difficult challenge. I feel that my occasional efforts to discreetly incorporate my experience into conversation— even when it seems highly relevant to do so—appear heavy-handed. And yet, I continue to try in the hope that such openness may enable me to further accept my own humanity while making others more aware. Who knows, perhaps my words may dispel stereotypes and in some small way soften hearts that are hardened to the inevitable suffering sexual trauma causes.

I believe that unarmed truth and unconditional love will have the final word in reality.
— MARTIN LUTHER KING, JR

PRACTICAL TIPS

1. By recognizing that the trauma is one of many parts of your loved one's identity, you give the survivor a sense of his or her wholeness, where no part is viewed as clandestine. And by allowing her or him the luxury of clumsiness when talking about this part, you help dissipate its power.

2. Often a victim feels the trauma has obliterated much of her or his personhood. In that case, kindly recall the many other experiences the survivor has had which prove otherwise. This will help to expand his or her self-image.

3. Family secrets are almost always destructive. When it comes to sexual crimes, the perpetrator ends up being protected while the victim is inadvertently punished. Why not heed the words of Jesus: "The truth shall set you free"?

4. With time, your loved one may be able to use her or his experience to help others who have suffered in the same way. Speaking out is a powerful healing tool, lessens the stigma of trauma, and affirms the strength of recovery. The decision to do this, however, can only be made by the survivor.

5. W.S. Merwin asked this question in his poem, "To The Sorrow String:" "What would the music be without

you?" This is a beautiful metaphor. Consider the possibility that the chorus of life is somehow mysteriously made richer because of the sorrow string.

chapter ten
BEGINNING AGAIN

Before ending Part One of this book, let us explore the ever-present and precious possibility of beginning. For each of us, this journey is essentially uncharted, so it is no wonder we frequently get lost. Surely, all of us have missed opportunities to show compassion, have constructed roadblocks on paths that might have led to reconciliation, and have selfishly, though not deliberately, withheld understanding to those we love. In my opinion, the adventure surrounding trauma is of mythic proportion, and the very effort to allow our best selves to shine forth despite the obstacles is in itself a heroic deed.

Beginnings allow for the possibility of new doors being opened. Even doors that have been slammed shut can be opened again. To those family and friends who have been negligent or worse, delinquent in your responses thus far, all is not lost. However, you need to be willing to repair the past if you seek to lovingly participate in the present. That means taking responsibility for misguided deeds and making amends. This is especially important if you have doubted the veracity of your loved one's story.

Though admitting one's mistakes is a difficult task, it is well worth the effort since the potential for healing is enormous.

This is best done in person, but if that is not possible, a letter or phone call is fine. (You may wish to refer to the sample letter in Chapter Two.) I can assure you from the many, many survivors I have interviewed, such generous gestures and displays of compassion are deeply appreciated. The challenge then for all of us becomes learning to let go of past failures. On both sides of the divide, we will fail. Forgiveness is the key, allowing us to move forward and begin afresh.

Time for another qualifier: because forgiveness is such a loaded and highly personal issue for those of us who have suffered sexual crimes, I want to be very clear that I am not speaking about the victim/perpetrator relationship here. I have only recently been able to forgive my father, and there are many who are never able to forgive their perpetrators. To do so or not to do so is strictly the victim's prerogative.

Returning now to the metaphor of physical injury discussed in the introduction, time, patience, and trying again and again are necessary steps to the rehabilitation of the spirit as well as the body. If you or your loved one is discouraged, remember that new occasions for healing will continually and often unexpectedly present themselves. Try to shine light on that little bit of magic. And if communication is strained, look for ways to soften the situation. My daughter and I have played a game where, if we have gotten into a fight and we cannot seem to find our way out of it, one of us will leave the room, re-enter, and we will begin again as if nothing had happened. I realize that is a simplistic solution and would be highly inappropriate for many of the painful and sometimes egregious situations in which we find ourselves. On the other hand, it is often much easier to begin anew than our pride would lead us to believe. We all have the power to offer the olive branch, and we can offer it repeatedly. Our higher selves bid us do so.

Finally, the ability to begin again is inextricably connected to hope and optimism, two essential components of the healing process. Rabbi Israel Ben Eliezer said, "The world is new each morning—that is God's gift and a man should believe he is reborn each day." Because sexual trauma carries with it a profound sense of loss, without some form of rebirth, optimism cannot be regained. We must continually reaffirm the very real possibilities for creating a good life in spite of all that was lost because of the trauma. After all, history abounds with examples of people who have suffered horrors and yet been triumphant. I count myself among those victors. And I also count the nineteen brave survivors who have contributed to this book among those victors. Why not your loved one? You can help.

I want to beg you as much as I can, to be patient toward all that is unsolved in your heart and to try to love the questions themselves like locked rooms and like books that are written in a very foreign tongue. And the point is, to love everything. Live the questions now. Perhaps you will then gradually, without noticing it, live along some distant day into the answers. Resolve to be always beginning—to be a beginner.

— RAINER MARIA RILKE

PRACTICAL TIPS

1. The trauma has already occurred and so, for most victims, the worst is over. All those clichés about today being the first day of the rest of your life are important reminders that though the past will inform the future, it need not defeat it.

2. For many survivors, religious rituals are glorious opportunities for regaining hope. The Jewish Day of Atonement, Yom Kippur, is profoundly rich in its healing potential. For Christians, the death and resurrection of Jesus is proof that nothing is impossible for God. Even the Sun Salutation practiced by yogis pays homage to the daily miracle of being alive.

3. If you have hurt your loved one through callous or judgmental behavior, words alone will not always eradicate wrongdoing. However, they can act as a very powerful starting point. If such words are offered with sincerity and love, seeds of restoration will be planted. You too can begin again.

4. Be optimistic for the victim. After years of serial romances and marriages, I stopped searching for a man to protect me and learned the liberating truth that I can actually protect myself. I have been alone now for over a decade, and, for the most part, I have done so fearlessly and joyfully. Part Two happily recounts other unforeseen victories.

5. For those we love, whose lives have been marred by trauma, may we continue to be heralds of brave beginnings and may our kindness be a sweet balm for their wounded hearts.

PART TWO:
OTHER VOICES,
OTHER PATHS

chapter eleven
SHAME: THE GLUE THAT BINDS US

Interviewing and selecting survivors for Part Two of my book has been nothing short of life-changing. Not only have I been able to see my wounds in the larger context of numerous other survivors, but by appreciating their courage, I have gained a sweeter appreciation for my own courage. I have also come to a greater understanding of the role that shame has played and continues to play in my life and the lives of others who have been sexually victimized.

Yet, this task of selecting has not been without formidable challenges. Many accounts were painful, powerful, and inspiring, yet because I sought to represent statistical realities, I had no choice but to reject a large number of very worthy candidates. Furthermore, it was essential to the goal of the book that victims be on the other side of the recovery process so as to affirm the real possibility of healing.

And not surprisingly, finding male survivors was much more difficult than finding females—not because they aren't out there, but rather because they are far less willing to acknowledge these injuries. Men who have been sexually abused or assaulted harbor complex feelings of having been emasculated whereas research suggests the gender identity of women who have been violated is usually not at risk. In a 2011 article in *Psychology Today*, Dr. Richard B. Gartner explains, "Masculine gender expectations teach boys they can't be victims. Boys are supposed to be competitive, resilient, self-reliant, and independent, but certainly not emotionally needy. 'Real' men initiate sexual activity and want sex whenever it's offered...For many men, these qualities define masculinity."[25]

Thankfully, these myths are being debunked, and more and more information regarding the prevalence and ramifications of male sexual trauma is becoming available. Again we see that when secrecy is eliminated, healing can begin. Unfortunately, we still have a long way to go in recognizing the widespread and too often ignored victimization of males.

Also problematic is the fact that it is impossible to adequately address the wide range of abuse and assault suffered by victims. There are by necessity many omissions but one of the more glaring for those who have been hurt in a spiritual context is Chapter Twelve, "Crimes of the Church." That chapter includes two survivors: one who was abused by a Catholic priest and one who was abused by a Christian youth minister. However, sexual crimes take place in all religious institutions.

Though the news of clergy abuse has been largely and justifiably focused on the Catholic Church, the Jewish community also has been flooded with scandals. And like the Catholic Church, *The New York Times* reported that among some ultra-orthodox Jews, there has been a systematic attempt to cover up these crimes.[26] Buddhism as well has been poisoned by its share of sexual abuse and assault allegations. Research carried out by the BBC Sinhala service has revealed that over the last decade, nearly 110 Buddhist monks have been charged for sexual and physical assaults on minors in Sri Lanka alone.[27]

Indeed, the far-reaching list of those culpable is sadly

endless, and no matter how many cases of sexual violence I could compile, such a compilation would be woefully incomplete. Even so, I maintain there exists a universality of shared pain between the majority of survivors that is profoundly reflected by the twelve women and eight men in this book and that the accounts presented will enable readers to gain whatever tools are required to effectively participate in the healing process of their loved ones.

Returning to the survivors selected, it is noteworthy that some of the experiences disclosed are more or less severe than others. This is deliberate. In fact, my biggest concern with Part Two is the fear that those victims, whose abuse was less extreme than the survivors in my book, might discount their own suffering. Anytime a sexual violation occurs there is the possibility of significant and long-term injury. In my own family, three victims of my father, who were geographically removed from him and did not suffer either the duration or extent of my abuse, nevertheless suffered deeply. As I mentioned in Chapter One, it is important to avoid making comparisons. I am speaking now as much to the victim as the support system because too many people have said to me over the years, "Oh, my abuse was nothing compared to yours." It is never "nothing." And in some instances, victims we might predict would have the hardest time healing and vice versa wind up surprising us. When we open our hearts, we begin to see that there are multiple unknown variables that contribute to a person's ability to overcome trauma, and we realize that all victims always are deserving of our support regardless of circumstances.

Present also in Part Two are three more survivors who suffered as I did from a dissociative memory disorder. According to the National Alliance on Mental Illness, a dissociative disorder is "an involuntary escape from reality characterized by a disconnection between thoughts, identity, consciousness, and memory...Dissociative disorders usually develop as a way of dealing with trauma."[28] Dr. Jim Hopper, researcher, clinician, and professor at Harvard Medical School, states, "Amnesia for childhood sexual abuse is a condition. The existence of this condition is beyond dispute."[29] Often called "a self-protection or survival technique because they allow individuals to endure 'hopeless' circumstances,"[30] dissociative disorders may last years depending on the severity of the trauma and the patient.[31] And though it is generally true that those suffering from acute dissociation have experienced prolonged abuse, my research indicates that there are many victims for whom that is not the case. Imagine, if you will, what it must be like for a child who is profoundly and morally betrayed by someone she or he trusts and who has no way of understanding the evil being done to her or him. Then ask, how does this child eat breakfast with that same person or see the perpetrator at family events and have the ego strength to incorporate such horror into the reality of day-to-day living? Depending on many variables, including the relationship of the perpetrator, the admonitions to remain silent, and the sensitivity of the victim, is it so difficult then to see that for many the only way to survive is through a splitting off from reality? The acclaimed researcher Dr. Jennifer Freyd, herself a victim of childhood sexual abuse and someone who suffered traumatic amnesia, is the author of many scholarly works including a stunning investigation entitled *Betrayal Trauma: The Logic of Forgetting Childhood Abuse*. For those who may still have questions, I commend it along with the following websites which provide in-depth information on the causes and consequences of dissociative disorders:

- jimhopper.com
- nami.org
- mentalhealthamerica.net
- isst-d.org

At the same time, I want to acknowledge that most people agree, including those who have dedicated their lives to helping victims of sexual abuse and assault, that there are rare instances when people have claimed to be victims of sexual crimes and then were found to be either deliberately lying or manipulated into believing something that was not true. We know that memory can be tampered with and we know that there are unscrupulous people in the world. However, it is egregious to scrutinize victims of sex crimes because of the deception of a few. "The big news is that we've shown how the human brain blocks an unwanted memory, that there is such a mechanism and it has a biological basis," says Stanford psychology professor John Gabrieli.[32]

These scientific findings are significant because, as you will read again and again from the survivors who share their experiences, being believed is critical to recovery. In fact, in my own life, and as a result of the research I have conducted, I have come to believe that nothing is more harmful to a victim than when he or she is not believed—or worse, called a liar.

The following amazing stories will serve to further illustrate the fact that survivors of sexual abuse and assault share many things in common. Victims often have major trust and intimacy issues, are hyper-vigilant, suffer from low self-esteem, battle depression, and have PTSD. However, I believe by far the worst thing about sexual trauma is that, in the large majority of cases, it causes a deep, pervasive, and persistent feeling of shame. Even though intellectually, we all know it is never the victim's fault, still victims too frequently blame themselves, and many struggle for long periods of time feeling damaged and dirty. Shame is the glue that binds us.

The Merriam Webster Dictionary defines shame as "a feeling of guilt, regret, or sadness that you have because you know you have done something wrong."[33] The Oxford Dictionary defines shame as "a painful feeling of humiliation or distress caused by the consciousness of wrong or foolish behavior; a loss of respect or esteem; dishonor."[34] Indeed, because victims of sexual crimes have been so deeply dishonored, they often feel that they themselves are dishonorable. In her lecture to the Department of Psychiatry at Harvard University entitled "PTSD as a Shame Disorder," Dr. Judith Herman, whose book *Trauma and Recovery* was referenced in Part One, explains: "At the Victims of Violence Program at Cambridge Hospital, where I work, the majority of our adult patients report histories of abuse in childhood…This breach… leaves our patients with the profound conviction that they are unlovable." She goes on to say that "Shame is a relatively wordless…acutely self-conscious state; the person feels small, ridiculous and exposed."[35] It is important not to confuse guilt with shame. As Dr. Brene Brown, who has researched the subject of shame for over a decade and is the author of *Daring Greatly*, said in her 2006 TED Talk, "Shame is a focus on self; guilt is a focus on behavior…Shame is 'I am bad,' and guilt is 'I did something bad.'" There is a huge difference between the two. Her research further revealed that "shame is highly correlated with addiction, depression, violence, aggression, suicide [and] eating disorders."[36]

Though there are many commonalities shared by victims, there is of course no cookie cutter behavioral response to either abuse or assault. Therefore, victims may act out their pain and shame in very differing ways—some more or less socially acceptable than others. But again, if we examine this from a heart place, it really doesn't matter. What matters is that we look to the root causes of these behaviors. Shame is a major root cause.

Sadly, this secret shame, this feeling of unworthiness and not being good enough, is a part—sometimes a daily part—of many victims' lives. And we who are engaged in a battle against shame are grateful to all who hold up a different mirror for us to look into. Having those who love us provide reality checks by reminding us of our strengths and assets is a most welcome counter to the distorted self-images many of us carry because of the trauma we suffered.

Unfortunately, there are many who do not survive the struggle. A complicated set of reasons accounts for this profound loss, but in my view, a lack of social support is frequently at the top of the list. And because this struggle is one that generally cannot be seen, and which victims bravely try to hide, it is essential that people understand it is nevertheless very real. Indeed, Mike Lew dedicates *Victims No Longer: The Classic Guide for Men Recovering from Sexual Child Abuse*, to (among others) "the memory of abuse victims who were overcome by the struggle." The tragedy of those words speaks volumes.

And yet—and this is an important "and yet"—as I mentioned in the conclusion of Part One, there are countless stories of victims who have not only overcome, but who have triumphed. On a positive note, Mr. Lew also dedicates *Victims No Longer* to "survivors as they recover and flourish." I am happy to say that the nineteen survivors who share their personal stories in this book are recovering and flourishing. They may still and perhaps always suffer the effects of the crimes committed against them, but each is on a path to recovery. These are people we would be lucky to call our friends, and they are doing wonderful things with their lives, many fully engaged in the task of helping others.

I want to encourage you, regardless of the specific reason you picked up this book, to read every survivor segment in every chapter whether it directly relates to your loved one or not. You will gain much from the collective wisdom of these strong men and women. Each shares from the heart stories of terrible wounds inflicted, followed by the often surprising and always inspiring miracle of healing that ensued. I am very proud to be among them.

It is one of the most beautiful compensations of this life that no man can sincerely help another without helping himself.

— RALPH WALDO EMERSON

chapter twelve
CRIMES OF THE CHURCH

DR. MARK MCALLISTER *resides in Vinton, Virginia. He works as a medical instructor at several colleges and as the SNAP (Survivors Network of those Abused by Priests) leader for Western Virginia. Dr. McAllister advocates for abuse survivors at the local, state, and national level. His perpetrator was convicted in 2014.*

I would like to consider myself a survivor today and no longer a victim. I am 44 years old and a divorced parent of two wonderful children. I spend my days trying to help young people make better lives for themselves through teaching and my nights trying to make a better life for myself through healthy living and healthy relationships. Growing up as an only child in a small Midwest town, I was in the vortex of the perfect storm for the abuser who indelibly changed my life. Father Gerald "Jerry" Howard was transferred to the Catholic parish to which my parents belonged when I was 12 years old. Jerry was a charismatic New Yorker in his thirties who rapidly gained the favor of the congregation, both adults and children alike. His persona attracted young boys through its paradoxical nature. He was a priest, yet he swore, smoked, and favored rock-n-roll music—things we were all experimenting with as we became teenagers. I was the ideal target for him in that my intelligence rather alienated me from my peers; I had an emotionally distant father and no siblings, and I lived by the church in which he ministered.

By the time I was thirteen, Jerry and I were spending a lot of time together. I fed off his eclectic wisdom and philosophies and his apparent selfless generosity. He confided in me that he had a similar "relationship" with another young boy in Jersey City and that sex was an integral part of their bond. The philosophy he fed me was that everyone at their core was bisexual and only the enlightened ones were able to acknowledge and embrace that. He expressed his hope that I might be such an enlightened individual and that we could relate on a similar level. When he later admitted to having been arrested in New Jersey for abusing a minor and said the church helped him legally change his name before relocation to my parish (while at the same time maintaining that he had done nothing wrong), I was already completely brainwashed. He started sexually abusing me that year and this continued under the same pretenses for the next five years.

What I endured during that time was perverse and horrific. Jerry was a large man and had a nasty temper. He used intimidation, fear, violence, shame, and addictive drugs to maintain my secrecy and silence. Abuse on so many levels by a person in a position of power and respect—and at the time when I was a boy transitioning into manhood—created many obstacles I would struggle to overcome. When the abuse ended and I was geographically distant from Jerry, I neither thought of nor spoke to anyone about it. In fact, I repressed all memories of what had happened for the next twenty years. But those twenty years were immensely troubled for me with recurrent substance abuse, sexual dysfunction, depression, unhealthy relationships, career interruptions, lack of spirituality, and an intense fear of men. My recollection of the abuse came in the form of "flooding" in my mid-thirties, sparked by the birth of my son. And it was shortly thereafter, while I was in a residential drug treatment center, that I disclosed for the first time what had happened to me.

Some of the first non-professionals I told of the abuse were my parents. Although my long history of troubles made them skeptical at first, they became my strongest supporters. My parents were devout Catholics, and I could tell it took an immense amount of resolve on their parts to abandon the church they loved in an effort to show solidarity with me. Although I never asked them to do this, it was a profound demonstration of their support. As I healed and began to take action against the church and the perpetrator, they were by my side during every proceeding, often taking ridicule from the church and answering to the media. Through the media, the story of my abuse became public, and many of my friends and schoolmates from that time became aware. The outpouring of support was energizing, and I began to discover that others were abused as well. Two of these individuals were brave enough to testify and make a criminal conviction of the perpetrator possible. Were it not for them, he may very well be abusing children even today.

During my rehabilitation, my family got me connected with David Clohessy and SNAP. Of all my supporters, no one has been more of a guiding light than David. His wisdom, experience, and most importantly, his genuine empathy were literally lifesaving. Coming out of the shadows of sexual abuse is overwhelming, and David was there tirelessly to guide me through my mental, emotional, spiritual, and legal issues. The fact that he was a survivor himself took away my ambivalence about sharing with others. When I cried, he cried;

when I laughed, he laughed; when I couldn't speak, he spoke for me. And therefore I trusted him implicitly. People ask me today how I found the courage to do some of the things I accomplished so soon after disclosing my abuse. The truth is I simply did what David told me to do.

In general, the support I received was truly liberating, but if I could change one thing it would be to lessen the fear that family and friends have expressed about asking me how I was doing during my early recovery or even today. People were always willing to talk about the status of the criminal cases, or other potential victims, or the reprehensible actions of the church, and I can certainly understand this being easier and racier conversation. However, most of my best "therapy" came from acceptance on behalf of friends and family when I discussed my rage, fear, disgust, jealousy, or sorrow. Same-sex abuse creates some tough questions and feelings in the young male victim. My best advice to supporters is to remember there is a person behind that tragedy who needs to feel accepted and loved, not judged.

And if love remains
Though everything is lost
We will pay the price
But we will not count the cost

— RUSH

LAURIE ASPLUND, the author of <u>Justice Before Mercy,</u> is a psycho-therapist in private practice working primarily with adolescents and their families. She has appeared on "Special Assignment" NBC, lectures at the University of Wisconsin, Whitewater on dialectical behavioral therapy, and is a citizen lobbyist advocating bills to prevent sexual violence.

I was raised in a close, upper-middle-class family with two loving parents and two older brothers. We lived in an idyllic resort town in Wisconsin, and my childhood was wonderful until the age of 14. That year, a "Christian" youth minister, who had ironically been hired to help us kids stay on the right track as we went through adolescence, targeted me, groomed me, and sexually abused me. He began by being my friend, making me feel special, and then introducing what he called "trust games." These games involved moving our hands up each other's legs ever so slowly towards our private parts and then stopping. During the next year and a half, his actions progressed to molestation, oral sex, and finally rape.

In the spring of 1976, when I was 16, my family moved to Iran. It was there, halfway around the world, that I finally told my family. Neither they nor I mentioned it to each other again. It was just too painful a topic, and none of us had the tools to address it. My parents felt guilty for not protecting me (as did my two older brothers), and I felt guilty for not only "allowing it to happen," but for not telling them sooner. Of course the reality is that these perpetrators are good at what they do. Their whole objective is to gain secret access to children, and sadly some become quite proficient at it.

It was only later in life, when I found a way to file criminal charges against my perpetrator 35 years after the fact, that we really discussed it as a family. What was so very helpful to me during this whole process, which began with reporting the decades-old crime and waiting for the district attorney to decide if he was going to prosecute, was the incredible validation and support that my whole family provided for me. That support ranged from lovingly listening whenever I needed to discuss the case or relay how I felt I was losing my mind to PTSD, to financially assisting me when I didn't have the strength to make it to work. My family also agreed to speak with the detective on the case, while surprisingly, other life-long friends didn't want to be involved.

Going into the process of seeking criminal justice, I knew it was going to be difficult because I would be asked the questions and hear the comments that victims fear the most: "Why did you let it happen?" "Why did it happen so many times?" "Why didn't you tell someone?" "You were old enough to know better, so you must have wanted it." "When asked if you were being sexually abused at the time, you answered no... Why?" These are all questions that we repeatedly ask ourselves because, even as victims, we don't always have the answers. Sexual abuse is such an insidious and predatory crime.

The criminal case lasted three years, and what I learned is that the people who are in charge of obtaining justice play very important parts in the healing process. I was fortunate to have a detective who was willing to let me work with him. I found out the name of one of my offender's previous victims and the detective graciously allowed me to contact her first so that I could try and soften the blow of what I was going to ask her. Fortunately she agreed to come on board, and that was the linchpin in the case. This was very difficult for her to do as she also had to go back in time to revisit what had happened. I can't thank her enough.

The district attorney was also wonderful. He believed me from the beginning and felt it was his duty to get justice for someone who was violated, no matter how long ago the abuse happened. And finally, the judge was an important piece in the healing process, not only to me, but to everyone else involved, as well as people within the community. He sentenced my perpetrator to ten years in prison.

Along with my family, my boyfriend Danny was extremely supportive during the case, although Danny has been supportive throughout the 30 plus years we have been together. From the beginning of our relationship, he knew of the abuse and would suggest fun activities to get my mind off the pain. We took trips together where he let me fish or be on my own for hours. He allowed me to rant, rave, complain, and cry. He helped me battle the warped view of sex that I had because of the abuse, always showing patience and intuitively knowing when I needed to be held or be left alone. He is my rock, my partner, and my best friend.

As a therapist, I believe that each person's life is like a jigsaw puzzle, and for whatever reasons, the pieces are jumbled up and not in place. My job is to identify all the pieces of the puzzle and help people put their lives back together. What I discovered through my court case was that a huge piece of my puzzle was missing, and because of this difficult journey that was shared by so many, that piece was found and put back into place, and as a result I finally feel whole.

I want survivors to know how important it is to speak

out and let people know you are suffering. It is crucial to healing. Sometimes you will not receive the support or validation you deserve, but know that there is a huge network of people who have also been victimized and are willing to help even total strangers. There is an invisible bond between us, born of shared pain and understanding, that unites us all.

Never apologize for showing feelings.
When you do so you apologize for the truth.
— BENJAMIN DISRAELI

chapter thirteen
ADULT SEXUAL ASSAULT

BECCA LYNN COURTRIGHT is is a member of The RAINN Speakers'
Bureau and the survivors' group Regain Your Voice. She has shared her story
on "Brave Miss World" and is currently writing a book entitled <u>Testify: My
Mission as a Rape Survivor</u>.

When we were 17, my twin sister, Beth, and I decided to run
track. The first weeks of training were brutal. I remember
during a difficult run, my legs felt full of cement, like I could
not run another step. Just as I slowed, Beth came running up
and put her arm around me and helped me to the finish line.
At the time, I did not realize the importance of her help or
how very much I would need it in the future.

It was 2003. I was 23 years old and was a newly divorced
single parent of my two-year-old son. One night, I got a flat
tire on a highway in Maryland. A man stopped to help me
change my tire. After convincing me the tire could not be
changed, he offered to give me a ride to a gas station. Once
in his car, he beat and raped me. I remember everything,
including yelling, "What if someone did this to your mother
or sister?" He got tired of me screaming and punched me in

my face until I was barely conscious. A strange feeling swept over me; I felt separated from my body as if I was floating above this scene, looking down on myself and my attacker. Once he was done with me, he started talking about whether or not he brought his knife. I was convinced he was going to kill me. A few minutes later, someone parked nearby and this caused my attacker to become erratic and panicked. I realized this was my chance to escape and managed to somehow get out of the car and run to a nearby construction trailer. A worker called 911, and my attacker, whom I later discovered was a serial rapist, fled.

The construction worker asked if I wanted to call someone. I called Beth, who was babysitting my son. I sobbed into the phone, "I got a flat tire and a man came and raped me." She screamed, "What? What do you mean?" After we got off the phone, she called my parents to let them know what happened and stayed overnight with my son. She waited till my son's daycare opened and then rushed to the hospital where I was surrounded by police and nurses.

Every day since, my twin sister has been the person I call if I have a bad day, if I have nightmares, or if I just need to remember it wasn't my fault. That day in high school represents how she has continued to support me even when I want to fall down.

Initially, I felt lost, alone, empty, and ashamed. I felt hopeless. I felt disconnected from my soul. My sister helped me by introducing me to new music and spending quality time with me. She treated me with respect, even when I did not feel like I deserved any. She called me after group therapy and asked how it went. Most of all, she listened. When I called, she listened without judgment. She accepted my journey as my own. She told me over and over that she loved me. She gave me reasons to recover and reminded me of all the beautiful things my life had to offer, most especially my little son.

Over the next nine years, I testified against my attacker in three trials. Beth stood by me during each one. She fielded questions from curious family and gave me space to focus on my testimony. With her by my side, I was strong enough to testify. She fought my fight with me, and it has made all the difference in my ability to heal.

I lost friends during my recovery. Not everyone was willing to deal with my journey. People I knew said it was not a big deal. They asked why I got in my attacker's car. They asked why I could not just move on. All of these insensitive comments made me feel isolated. It made me feel they did not understand the real impact of my rape. I also experienced some people who didn't want to believe horrible things like this could happen. They felt safer denying the truth. It was easier for them to blame me.

My advice to family of victims is to give them grace to grieve at their own pace. Recovery is a slow process. The victim might act cold, removed, or lost. Your job is to hold that person tight and not let her or him feel alone. Make victims feel safe and let them know you will never abandon them. Show them all the things they loved before. Provide a stress-free environment. Take care of any responsibilities that might make them worry. The main job for victims is to re-connect with their souls, to repair themselves, and to forgive themselves. Your job is to remind them of the amazing life they still have waiting for them.

Another way to help victims is to look them in the eyes. People naturally avoid looking into the eyes of someone in distress and instead look down or away. Looking people straight in the eyes shows that they are being seen and not being judged. This tells them they need not feel ashamed and that you are present and willing to support them however you are able.

I was forever changed by my attack, but I was fortunate to have my twin who held me up when I could not move forward. I attribute much of my recovery to her unwavering support and wish that every survivor could have that kind of support. Finally, I remind myself over and over that I will never let one night define the rest of my days.

Give me hope in the darkness that I may see the light.

— MUMFORD & SONS

PRESTON DECORTE is a career officer in the United States Armed Forces. Though his assault was not military-related and was perpetrated by a civilian, his story was shared at a 2013 military training on sexual assault and prevention. Preston is also a member of The RAINN Speakers' Bureau.

Following my commission as a United States Naval Officer at the age of 26, I was stationed at a training command in Georgia. In May 2010, a few of my civilian buddies, some acquaintances, and I went on a weekend kayaking trip. After kayaking, we headed up to a cabin in the mountains. It was a great place and we were all having a good time. Eventually everyone went into the cabin to watch TV, but I stayed on the porch and had a few drinks alone. One of the men who I did not know well came outside and began talking and drinking with me. He was making the drinks, and a few hours later I was throwing up.

At about 0230, I felt someone's hand fondling my genitals and a leg between mine. Frozen in disbelief, I first thought I was dreaming. When I opened my eyes and realized it was real, I wanted to kill him. I asked God to guide me to do the right thing, and I believe his spirit got me out of the cabin. I grabbed my things, left the cabin, and ran barefoot through the woods and down the mountain for at least two miles before I was able to get a ride. I had to make a choice to either attack the attacker or to leave. I carry guilt everyday that I left without hurting him and feel less of a man because of it.

I immediately reported it to my command the next morning and was guided to receive the help I needed. When I went to the local Sexual Assault Civilian Center, the first thing the counselor told me was, "I'm so happy you showed up because this just happened to you and you're a male." She explained to me that victims, especially males, often do not speak up because of the shame.

Looking back, I wish I had pressed charges, but I was moving in a few months and I knew that it was highly unlikely that justice would be done. According to the Rape, Abuse, and Incest National Network, 60 percent of sexual assaults are not reported to the police. For the 40 percent that do get reported, ten lead to an arrest, eight get prosecuted, four lead to a felony conviction, and only three will end up in prison. These are disheartening numbers, but still there are days when I regret that decision.

I've told a number of people about my assault and have heard the right things, the wrong things, and have even seen the blank stares. Throughout my journey, there have been many people who have helped me. I told one of my friends about the assault a few hours after it happened, and without hesitation she said, "Preston, I want you to know that this is not your fault. This person is a monster and this was his own sick desire to gain power over you. You did everything right last night, and I am so proud of the man that you are and to call you my friend." She then went on to share with me her experience of having been abused, and that opened my eyes to a whole new world of victims helping victims. When we tell people we love about this event, it's not that we're looking for them to solve the problem; we just want to know that we are still accepted and loved.

A year ago following the news of numerous military sexual assaults, every command was tasked with completing sexual assault and prevention training. I wrote my story and emailed it to my commander. The next morning he came by my desk and asked me to his office. He said, "Preston, I received your e-mail last night, and you know I had to stop three times while reading it because I began to tear up. You just never know who this happens to." He went on to tell me about victims he's known and thanked me for sharing my story, and later that afternoon, he read it at our sexual assault and prevention training. It had been three years since my assault, and I sat there in a room with over thirty service members thinking to myself, *That's me, that's my story*, and it felt good to hear it and to witness the discussion that followed. It was an empowering moment and one that I will continue to take with me.

With those who have helped me have also come those who have hurt me. Following my assault, I texted a friend about what had happened. Her response was "Did he think you were gay?" I am not gay, but why would anyone ask a victim about sexual orientation instead of just showing compassion? Another friend I told about the assault said, "What made him think he could do that to you? He must have thought there was a reason he could do that." These responses triggered feelings of anger and hurt. I always hate hearing people start a question with "Why?" Victims of sexual trauma shouldn't feel like they need to defend themselves when seeking comfort. An assault occurred; whatever took place prior never justifies one person assaulting another.

Though I am still haunted by what happened, I have learned to deal with it and have been able to help other assault victims, both in the military and civilians. Some days I feel empowered and other days I feel like I've taken three steps back. My mom, who has been one of my main supporters, told me that I have nothing to feel guilty about, and I know what she is saying is true. In time, I will believe it in my heart, and then I will be free.

Use the pain as fuel, as a reminder of your strength.
— AUGUST WILSON

chapter fourteen
ABUSE BY A SIBLING

RENA ROMANO *is the author of* <u>His Puppet No More</u>*, co-author of the best seller* <u>World Class Speaking In Action</u>*, a professional keynote speaker, and a certified speaking and personal empowerment coach. Rena had the great honor of sharing her story on "The Oprah Winfrey Show."*

Today I am a professional speaker and a speaking and leadership coach, but I remember the day I lost my voice to someone I loved and trusted. When I was four years old my half brother, who is eleven years older than me, began sexually abusing me. The abuse lasted for twenty years and kept me in an internal hell I fought to get out of, but didn't know how to escape. At four, I didn't even understand what was happening.

As a teen I was forced to do drugs and pornography. He bullied me and made me feel unworthy and ashamed. He also silenced me with gifts and secret promises. No one knew what I was going through. I could have won an Oscar for my deception because I wanted so desperately to appear significant, worthy, and happy. But I wasn't happy; I was dying a slow death every time he touched me. And yet, I was terrified to tell anyone, certain that if I did, I would be blamed, or he would be blamed and punished, and then he would punish me.

Completely brainwashed by his manipulations, I actually felt that my other two brothers didn't love me because they never tried to have sex with me. (Years later when I told them how I felt, they both fell to their knees and cried out in rage wanting to kill him. It was consoling to know that they loved me as brothers should and wanted to protect me.)

As time passed, I became suicidal and immobilized by panic attacks. Even after I was able to stop the abuse by moving to another state, the symptoms of abuse continued with alcohol, drugs, and men. I tried to deaden my silent pain any way that I could.

When I finally found the courage to tell my mother and other siblings, they were devastated but they rallied to protect me. I had been so afraid to break my silence and yet they immediately flew me home to be with them, to care for me physically and emotionally. My family believing me was crucial to my healing—I know this. They believed every word and didn't question any of the shocking details I shared with them. They listened, allowing me to cry and talk, without interruption or judgment.

In my therapy group, most of the women didn't have the support I received. Some were blamed, others called liars; a few were kicked to the curb when they told their mothers who then allowed their perpetrator to remain in the home. It was heart-wrenching to see their torment, and I felt guilty that they didn't have the same support I did. It is so important for survivors to be believed and allowed to share their experiences openly and honestly with family and friends. This is vital to our individual healing process, and without it, recovery is incredibly difficult, if not impossible.

After my visit with my family, I met with my best friend.

I shared the positive experience I received from my family and how helpful it was. She abruptly said, "Why don't you just get over it and stop talking about it?" I was shocked and saddened that she was unsupportive, and as a result, the friendship ended. I have witnessed many survivors lose friends when they try to share their pain.

When I met my husband I wanted him to know exactly what he was getting into. I told him everything and he allowed me to talk, once again without interruption or judgment. From the beginning, I have felt safe with him. He encouraged me to write my memoir because somehow he knew that writing about my experience would help me release the demons that still lingered. And so it did. The panic attacks and thoughts of suicide are long gone, but there are residual effects that I still deal with, and my husband knows and accepts them.

Over the years I have shared my story in speeches and in conversations. I have been met with different reactions. The ones that have been most disturbing are: "Just get over it," "You talk too much about it," "You shouldn't talk about it because it will hurt your business." On the positive side, I have been hugged and thanked and told how brave I am and that I am obligated to talk about it to help others. I admit I like hearing that, because I refuse to ever be silenced again.

Did he murder the person who could have been? Probably. Who knows? I don't dwell on that because I have forgiven. What I do know is that it will always be a part of me, and I accept that because I finally love the woman I have become. I am a public speaker, a published writer, an advocate, a wife, and a friend, and I am making a difference. Whenever I share my story, inevitably someone comes to me and whispers, "That happened to me, but I am afraid to talk about it," "I haven't found my voice yet," "I have kept my abuse a secret because I feel so ashamed and guilty." I am honored that these women and men trust me and I encourage all of them to seek help, to tell others, and to write about what happened to them. I tell them the truth: recovery is not easy work, but it's absolutely worth it. If you break your silence you can learn to heal, and you too can find your voice.

I can be changed by what happens to me.
But I refuse to be reduced by it.
— MAYA ANGELOU

CALLEN HARTY *is the author of 23 plays, including the autobiographical* Invisible Boy, *and two books* My Queer Life *and* Empty Playground: A Survivor's Story. *Callen is also the organizer of the survivor conference "Paths to Healing" and speaks regularly about recovery.*

The first time my oldest brother abused me I was ten years old. It began with a grope through my pants, and when I told my mother she said, "Oh, you shouldn't let him do that to you." Her response only caused me to feel more ashamed than I already was, so when something more profound happened, I didn't bother trying to tell her. Besides, my brother, who was six years older than me, had warned me not to tell anyone. The abuse continued until I was almost 18 (even after he was married and had children) and included molestation, oral sex, and rape.

As a result of the abuse, I suffered many of the standard symptoms, including depression, alcoholism and drug abuse, promiscuity, low self-worth, suicidal ideation and attempts, dissociation, and PTSD. While I am generally healthy now, there are still triggers that can bring certain emotions flooding back. This year marked 25 years without a drink and even longer without other drugs.

It is important for family and friends to realize that sexual abuse in childhood alters one's entire life. The body is abused but so are the heart and mind. Generally, both the abuse and the pain are kept secret, but these secrets inform everything. Trust is broken, and unhealthy coping mechanisms are often acquired in an effort to survive. I really hit some lows and threw away a lot of potential for quite some time. While I have worked hard to make up for the loss and have many accomplishments, I sometimes wonder how much more I might have done with my life had the abuse never happened.

For victims, I believe the most important parts of healing are accepting the profound impact the abuse has on one's life, sharing the story, working to move past the hurt, and trying to turn the pain into something positive. Family and friends can be helpful in all parts of the process. With each trusted loved one with whom the story is shared, the acceptance of it becomes easier. When it is shared, it becomes more real but has less power. When it is held inside, it eats away. Sharing can take many forms, but I believe that healing is virtually impossible without it.

I have been fortunate to have people who cared about me and allowed me to share my pain. The first was my friend Laurie in high school. We were both about 17, and when I told her, she listened and believed me, which was more important than anything else at that time. Another was a housemate, Lauren, who lived in the same co-op as I did and to whom I was able to turn when I was feeling very suicidal. I saw the light on in her room and knocked. Lauren opened the door and invited me in where I sat and cried for a long, long time. With kindness and compassion, she allowed me to let go of so much through those tears. It wasn't until years later that I shared with Lauren what was behind my pain and how close I had come to taking my life that night.

The other important people in my recovery have been my friend Sunshine, my sister Coleen, and my life partner

Brian whom I have been with for 23 years. They have all allowed me to share my story, believed me, and lovingly listened without judgment. I wasn't looking for advice or platitudes; I just needed to get my story out, and they let me do that. The few things they did say included helpful things like, "I'm sorry that happened to you," "What can I do for you?" or "I want to help you, but I don't know how." These supportive comments showed me that they were there with me and that my story didn't make me a horrible person in their eyes. They still listen when I need to talk—which isn't all that often as I tend to process a lot on my own and through my writing—but I know they're with me. And hugs are always good for me, and they're great at that too.

Unfortunately, I believe people frequently don't know how to deal with the subject of sexual abuse. It took me years to realize that my mom, who was widowed when I was two, simply did not know what to say when I told her what happened to me. Of course I wish she had said, "He shouldn't do that," and then had done something to make sure it didn't happen again. But she came from an era when these things weren't talked about, and I don't think she had a clue how to handle it. Even now, people are afraid of the subject. I find that whenever I post something online about child sex abuse, the posts rarely get "likes" or comments. People prefer not to be reminded about what an epidemic it is.

In 2008 after suffering a life-threatening heart attack, I decided it was important to share my story further, and I wrote my play, *Invisible Boy*, which was produced in both Madison and San Antonio. In Madison, we had powerful talkbacks after the shows, where audience members unburdened themselves with their own stories after hearing mine. Since then, I have accepted many speaking engagements and have organized an annual conference on surviving childhood sex abuse that focuses on male survivors. It's called "Paths to Healing," and it lets others know they are not alone. It lets me know I am not alone.

Finally, for me—and this isn't for everyone—I also had to come to a place of forgiveness because the anger and hatred inside me were destroying me, not my perpetrator. Forgiveness doesn't mean that what happened was okay. It simply means that I was no longer going to hold on to it. I was going to let it go.

No person is your friend who demands your silence,
or denies your right to grow.

— ALICE WALKER

KELLY HAYES is a Reiki Master, licensed massage therapist, and a certified Hatha yoga teacher. She also has a master's degree in psychology and is a volunteer for the RAINN Speakers' Bureau. Kelly took her brother to court in 2008 where he was sentenced to eight months in prison and put on the sex offender registry.

I am an incest survivor, having suffered sexual abuse at the hands of my biological brother. He is seven years older than me and molested me from the ages of 4 to 16. When I was 21, I finally came forward and told people what happened.

Before sharing my story with you, I think it's important to try and answer a question that almost everyone asks or is at least thinking: "Why wait so long to say something?" Well, growing up and being molested is a horribly confusing tragedy for any child. My abuse was by my brother, and I was taught to trust my family and that my family members were the people who would love and take care of me. A young child's mind is not fully developed and does not have the same reasoning powers as an adult, and when sexual abuse occurs, normal cognitive development is thwarted. There is also a conflict between the body and the mind. The body, biologically speaking, responds to sexual pleasure, whereas the mind knows something's amiss. This causes further confusion, guilt, and shame, and these feelings, along with a fear of reprisal, are deeply conflictual and inhibiting to victims. Why I waited is a very painful question for me, and that is the best answer I can give. I think I can speak for most victims when I say we would be better off if we were not asked any question that begins with "why," but hopefully I have shed some light on the issue.

When I finally got up the courage to speak out, the first people I confided in were my best friend, her family, and my uncle. I was a mess then because everything that had been bottled up for so long was finally coming out. My uncle was amazing; he cried with me, called me regularly to see how I was doing, made me laugh, and invited me to family events. I never felt shamed or judged by my uncle.

Soon after my uncle, I told my parents. They immediately believed me, saying they trusted my confession because I had always been a truthful individual. I was very fortunate in this respect, as so many people in these situations are not believed. I know it was hard for my parents because the perpetrator was their son, and I never expected them to shun my brother. What I did expect was to get their emotional support. I wanted them to hug me and acknowledge how terrible it was and to tell me they were sorry for not protecting me. Instead, their acceptance of the truth was immediately followed by their demand that I not tell anyone because it was "a family matter" and could be fixed by the family. What they did not realize, however, is being told to keep it a secret after I had kept it a secret my whole life only added to my incredible shame and pain.

A year later, I took my brother to court. I will never forget walking into the courtroom and finding my parents sitting on my brother's side and never once making eye contact with me. The judge sentenced my brother to eight months in prison. I remember feeling guilty for having him arrested as I watched him being taken away in handcuffs, even though he yelled at me during the proceeding when the judge asked him to apologize to me. Still, justice was done, and that was the proudest day of my life.

My parents and sister did not speak to me for seven years. And sadly, my uncle stopped talking to my father (his brother) for a long time. I could see the sadness in my uncle's eyes when this happened. But in the last year, we have all reunited, and our relationships are now based upon love, honesty, and deep respect for one another. I have forgiven myself, and I think they have forgiven themselves, and we are now able to live in the present instead of the past. Although I still do not have contact with my brother and am unsure if I ever will, I hope some day we can make amends.

A wonderful thing happened a year after the verdict; I met the man I would marry. And though the relationship ultimately did not last, he helped me during a very crucial time in my life when my own family had rejected me. I have always and still do struggle with emotional intimacy with people, and I continue to suffer from symptoms related to the abuse. Nevertheless, I am confident that I will keep on healing and that in time I will again experience love in my life.

Today, I consider myself a survivor instead of a victim. I listen to my feelings and allow them to guide me, and I am happy to say that for the most part I am going in the right direction. Now when I share my story, it is not to get sympathy, but rather to inspire others. I want to show that there is always hope and to encourage people to come together in times of heartache, no matter how difficult it may be.

Peace: it does not mean to be in a place where there is no noise, trouble, or hard work. It means to be in the midst of those things and still be calm in your heart.

— UNKNOWN

chapter fifteen
PATERNAL PERPETRATORS

TEDD CADD is a retired Coast Guard Officer currently working as the financial manager for Alongside Ministry International. Since 1992, he has also been a strong advocate for sexual abuse survivors, volunteering as a trained group leader for "Journey Groups," a product of Open Hearts Ministry in Kalamazoo, MI. He is also part of The Bristle Cone Project.

It took 22 years before I could believe my wife loved me. I have been fairly successful, but that success has been accompanied by a deep sense that I was damaged and would be found out. As a result, it has been difficult for me to try new things or to express my desires or to just have fun. I've been a good dad, but it came at a cost. I had to study and learn what it meant to be a good dad.

The reason I had to study how to be a good dad is that I never had a role model. My own father sexually abused me from the time I was five until I was twelve years old. He also abused his own sister and two of his brother's daughters (my cousins). No one ever talked about it. His threat to kill me with his .38 revolver if I ever told anybody was sufficient to ensure my silence. I feel certain my emotionally abusive mother knew and chose not to protect me. When I finally told her decades later, she showed no surprise and offered no apologies.

For years, I suffered from recurring nightmares, isolation, hyper-vigilance, flashbacks, traumatic amnesia, dissociation, and distrust. I still don't trust men in general. But the worst was the terrible shame that made me feel I was too dirty to be loved.

I often wonder how different my life would have been if someone had spoken up. Just recently, I found a letter from my dad's sister confronting him about what he had done to her as a child. In that letter she says she still feels guilty for not saying something so he wouldn't have been able to abuse others.

Without a doubt the thing that helped me most as a kid was my membership in a local church. Even though the people at the church had no clue about what was going on in my family, they knew Jesus and that was what I needed the most. My faith in a loving God has been an anchor for me my whole life.

One of the effective people at the church was Jim. He was an adult mentor during my senior year that made me feel safe. Jim knew nothing about my history but he accepted me and showed me what a real family is like. When my parents got divorced, he even invited me to go with his family to the church family camp. That meant the world to me. One irony of this: years later, after I was largely healed from the abuse, I told Jim the general story. Then I asked him how he felt about it. He said that his first thought was about when he was molested on a playground as a child. I wonder what would have happened if I could have trusted him enough to tell him. It's so important that we encourage kids to speak up.

Despite the cruelty of my childhood, I married a

wonderful woman. Pam and I have been together forty-five years, and she has been my greatest supporter. Still, the healing process is so very painful at times. Initially, I trusted Pam with only small parts of the story, and she didn't throw me away. So when I started confronting the abuse in earnest, I felt like I could trust her with more. When I finally told her the ugliest parts (even giving her permission to read my journals), Pam not only accepted me, but held me in her arms and comforted me. When someone knows the very worst parts of your history and still cares about you, that is incredibly healing.

In 1992, I became an advocate for sexual abuse victims, doing multiple trainings to learn as much as I could, taking crisis calls, and making hospital visits. I have also been leading groups for abuse survivors since 2005. Through these experiences, I have learned a lot and I share some key things here in hopes that they may be useful for those people who want to help other survivors:

- Get familiar with the facts about sexual abuse and its effects. There are a number of resources available. My favorite is Dr. Dan Allender's book *The Wounded Heart*.

- Remember that it is not your job to tell victims what they need to do to heal.

- Communicate to them that you will keep their story in <u>complete</u> confidence.

- Realize that you may be the brunt of some anger. Steady yourself to hear some ugly things and decide beforehand that you are going to accept those things without reacting.

- Respond not with questions but with affirming comments.

- The more you are able to lovingly sit with somebody in a place of heavy grief without trying to make that person snap out of it, the better friend you will be.

- Research counselors and therapists in your area who are knowledgeable about sexual abuse and have those resources available to share with the survivor.

- Most importantly, be a supportive listening ear. Nothing is more healing for survivors than being heard and validated.

It has taken a long time, but I thank God that today I am able to receive love and to give love. It is love after all that has healed my wounds. I can share this love with Pam, my children, my grandchildren, and with other survivors.

The tongue that brings healing is a tree of life.
— PROVERBS 15:4

KATHY PICARD is the recipient of numerous awards including the 2014 Pynchon Award, the Zonta Founder's Day Award, the 2013 Public Policy Advocacy Award from the Massachusetts Office for Victim Assistance, and the 2010 Honoree for Massachusetts Missing Children's Day. She partners with YMCA and Girl Scouts teaching "Childhelp: Speak Up Be Safe" and tirelessly works to change legislation affecting children.

I am one of the lucky ones because I am a strong survivor who has been able to turn my biggest tragedy into my biggest victory. An advocate and educator for the prevention of sexual abuse, I am fortunate to talk about my personal story and teach others about this still silent epidemic.

From the young age of seven until I was seventeen, I was sexually abused by my stepfather. I didn't realize what I was going through or even that what he was doing was wrong. He told me it was a form of love, and I believed him. As a young girl, I would pull out my eyelashes and eyebrows and faint often. Throughout my teens and twenties, trust was a huge issue; I didn't trust the words that people said to me, and I thought those close to me were cheating on me. This abuse has and will always be a part of my life, but it no longer defines me.

Two people who have really helped me in my healing are my Aunt Judy (for being the mom to me I didn't have) and my husband Gary. When I finally spoke out, after the abuse ended, I went to my Aunt Judy. She let me share everything that happened and gave me love, comfort, and support. My Aunt Judy was always there. Unfortunately she told me—and even made me promise—never to tell anyone for fear of what her brother-in-law would do. But still, just knowing I could talk to her, that she believed me, understood me, and loved me as her own daughter, made all the difference. My own mother was never a mother to me. I wish she had been able to admit what actually happened rather than choosing her husband over me and telling others that I was lying and looking for attention. Her words were very hurtful, but I know the truth.

Anyway, I kept my promise to my Aunt Judy until she died in 2000, but after that I spoke out, and I have been speaking out ever since. And on November 5, 2015, I got my justice! After a three-day trial, an eight-member jury found in favor of plaintiff Kathy Picard in the case 3:14-cv-30115 Picard v. Buoniconti. It is the only case of its kind to go to trial in federal court in Springfield. Happily, because I won the case against my stepfather, I was also instrumental in changing the statute of limitation laws in Massachusetts to the age of 53 (my age at the time of the trial). It has been a long battle.

My husband Gary has made my past much easier to accept because I have someone that I can always talk to about how I am feeling. Gary is my soul mate, and when I am triggered and experience PTSD, he shows understanding and compassion. He knows my strengths and weaknesses, and he supports me through it all. I want to encourage victims to believe that real love is possible. Because survivors often feel ashamed and even like they are "damaged goods," they may feel like they have to settle, but this is not so. Take your time. I was 35 when I got married, and I am so glad that I waited!

Another important person in my life is retired Chief of Police Lou Barry. For the past six years this caring man has invited me to come to the Police Academy to educate his students. This is not only healing for me, but hopefully prepares future police officers in the ways that they can help victims of sexual crimes.

In addition to teaching, I am mentoring a 16-year-old who was also sexually abused. That too is healing as it allows me to give to her what I wish I had been given. I would like to share some things that I do to help this wonderful young person—things I wish all survivors could experience:

- When I see that she is struggling or having a hard day, I make a point of asking her if she wants to talk about what is bothering her. Some days she may and some not. It's important to be available but not to pressure someone to talk.

- I send her small gifts, surprises in the mail for no reason at all, or a text saying, "Thinking about you," or "Tomorrow will be a better day." These little things let her know I care.

- I let her know that I will listen to anything she needs to talk about and that nothing she says or does will ever cause me to go away.

And finally, I want to share with parents and caregivers how critical it is to educate children as young as possible. In *Childhelp: Speak Up Be Safe* I explain to children the importance of using the correct names for their body parts. This can potentially save a child from abuse. For example: a child calls her

vagina a "cookie" and tells a teacher, "He touched my cookie."
Sadly, disclosures are often missed because children don't
know the right words to use. Having a Childhelp program
(www.childhelp.org/speak-up-be-safe-for-educators) in a
community can make a big difference. Also, there is a wonderful book entitled *My Body Belongs To Me* by Jill Starishevsky
for three- to five-year-olds that I recommend.

Everyone can help, including you and me. When I was
that young girl pulling out my eyelashes, I never would have
believed that one day I would receive *The Unsung Heroine of the
Massachusetts Commission on the Status of Women Award*. Senator Gale
Candaras presented me with the award in 2006, and in her
speech she quoted John F. Kennedy:

One person can make a difference, and everyone should try.

chapter sixteen

ASSAULT WITHIN THE MILITARY

BRIAN LEWIS is the first male survivor of military sexual trauma to testify about the issue before the Senate Armed Services Committee and the House Committee on Veterans' Affairs. He is president of Men Recovering from Military Sexual Trauma, an advisory board member of Protect Our Defenders, and an administrator of menthriving.org.

I had a good childhood. I played baseball, I bowled, and I had a loving family. I enrolled in the Junior ROTC program at Meade Senior High School and was the Cadet Battalion Commander of the Mustang Battalion there in 1996. I chose to enlist in the United States Navy right after high school for the educational benefits and a chance to see the world. I enjoyed those first few years in the Navy. I made good friends, saw a lot of places I wouldn't have seen otherwise, and learned a lot about myself. In the spring of 2000, I was transferred from Hawaii to Guam.

I was raped in Guam while serving aboard the USS Frank Cable (AS-40) in August of 2000. After the rape, a senior member of the command ordered me not to file a report with the Naval Criminal Investigative Service. I then found out that my perpetrator was a serial predator, having committed these acts against other members onboard the same command. I was sent back out to sea aboard the Cable after the rape. When the psychiatrist realized I couldn't perform my duties, I was medically evacuated on a litter with four point restraints under chemical sedation to Naval Medical Center San Diego. The psychiatrist there accused me of lying about the rape and diagnosed me with a personality disorder. I received a general discharge from the Navy one year after the rape.

I fell into a deep depression after my discharge. I tried to commit suicide. I tried to drink the memories away. I tried to make the outside of my body feel like the inside through cutting and overeating. I attempted to get my discharge corrected and failed. I survived domestic violence during this period. The Veterans Health Administration sent me to a mixed gender residential recovery program at Bay Pines, Florida that harmed more than it helped. Then things began to change.

My greatest saving grace thus far has been my spouse. We met in 2008 and were married on June 27, 2015. He is a very gentle and caring person and has continually reminded me that the abuse was not my fault. At the same time, he's never let me use post-traumatic stress as an excuse for doing something wrong or not trying my best. He taught me that post-traumatic stress is not a "get out of jail free card" for when trouble rears its head. He strongly encouraged me to return to school and seek undergraduate and graduate degrees. Education can be a very powerful tool for survivors because it opens up the possibility for a better future. When I had a medical procedure that was heavily triggering, he was the one who stayed with me and comforted me through that difficult experience. I truly believe his actions are instrumental in helping me to find a path instead of a circle in my recovery process. He also helps me realize that what happened in the past is not necessarily what will happen in the future and to react to what is happening in the here and now. He does this through a lot of grounding techniques taught in dialectical behavior therapy. Our partners rarely receive enough credit, but many of us could not do the things we do without them. Indeed, family and friends can be the lifesavers of the survivor.

My next saving grace has been reestablishing old friendships and building new ones—friends I had from the Navy before the rape like Dan Larkin and Jeff Sarnecky who never knew the full story about what happened but when they found out, sent me emails and made phone calls to tell me that they wished they had been there to help me. I am also grateful to friends I have met in my advocacy work who stand in solidarity with me as a survivor. And through my recovery work, I have learned how to talk to friends I've hurt and to make amends. True friends will always stand beside you, and survivors are capable and deserving of having true friends.

Where am I today? Well, I've earned my bachelor of science degree in paralegal studies and my master of science in forensic studies. I'm currently a second year student at Mitchell Hamline School of Law where I am pursuing a joint juris doctor and master of arts in public administration. I'm also a Freemason. Besides my earlier testimonies (mentioned in my bio), I have testified in front of other congressionally chartered panels looking into sexual assault in the military, and I have submitted written testimony to Congressional hearings regarding sexual assault in the military and the substandard treatment male survivors receive from the Veterans Health Administration.

You might think I'm tooting my own horn. Not so much. This advocacy thing ain't about me; it's about helping my brothers and sisters in uniform. To the other survivors, I ask you to get active. I want you to see that hope is out here, recovery is out here. I want you to step forward. I want you to share your stories. There is a diverse community of military sexual trauma survivors and partners waiting for you to join us. I can only make one promise about how it will go:

When we go into battle, I will be the first to set foot on the field, and I will be the last to step off, and I will leave no one behind. Dead, or alive, we will all come home together.
— LTG HAROLD "HAL" MOORE, USA (RET.).

JESSICA HINVES *serves on the advocacy board of Protect Our Defenders and was featured in the Oscar- and Emmy-nominated documentary "Invisible War." She has advocated for military sexual trauma survivors, appearing on numerous television and radio broadcasts including PBS News Hour, Nightline, Katie Couric, and NPR.*

I was born and raised in northern Kentucky and moved to east Texas where I worked at a vineyard, owned my own little country home, and attended community college before I joined the Air Force in 2007. I come from a military family and was a jet mechanic on F-15 C, D, and E models. It was at Nellis Air Force Base in Nevada in 2011 before a deployment that an airman I worked with broke into my bathroom and raped me. I reported the assault and there was a yearlong investigation, which led to a recommendation from JAG (Judge Advocate General) for an Article 32 hearing. Two days before the court hearing, my attacker's commander dropped all charges and told me, "He didn't act like a gentleman, but there isn't any reason to prosecute."

Today, I am a full-time stay-at-home mother, and my husband Scott is on active duty. We have two beautiful children, Patrick (four) and Marley (three) and a puppy named Bob Barker, but I continue to suffer almost daily from the trauma I experienced.

My husband and I met each other during our Air Force training. We were in the same class together and soon became good friends. After the assault, I completely lost who I was and felt shattered and overwhelmed to the point of suicide. I called Scott (not yet my husband), and when I told him what happened, he drove straight from his base in another state to mine and immediately became my biggest advocate. He reassured me of who I really am and affirmed that I had been a dedicated crew chief and that none of this was my fault. He was unflinching in his support and remained my faithful comrade despite the growing crowd of people who did not believe that I was actually raped. My rapist had been given the Airman of the Quarter award during the investigation, and the truth is that if this hadn't happened to me, I never would have believed it myself.

I was transferred to my soon-to-be husband's base because my truck was tampered with and I was receiving death threats. Scott showed me around base and always made me feel protected. I had a few panic attacks the first few days, and he drove me to the base hospital and sat with me the entire time. Then four months after my transfer I was discharged from the military for having PTSD. It is very painful for me that I was kicked out of the military because I suffered PTSD while the person who assaulted me and caused my PTSD did not even have to face charges for his crime.

Scott and I eventually got married, and as time went on, he realized the PTSD wasn't going away. As a result, he felt helpless and withdrew. This in turn created a wedge between us and hurt our marriage. We got counseling and learned ways to work together. One of the best things Scott does now is encourage me to get outdoors. We go for bike rides and walks and hikes. Scott finds used exercise equipment online for cheap and we try to eat healthy. All of these things have helped tremendously and enabled me to get off medication. Yoga especially, but exercise in general, makes me feel comfortable in my body and more open to intimacy. And roller Derby helps me feel empowered and release anger. And yet, there are still times when Scott comes home from work and has to take the kids because I am so depressed or suffering from anxiety. My husband and I just returned to counseling to learn more skills and are planning to attend a couples' retreat next year. Scott is also looking into support groups to help him with the difficult task of being a caregiver.

My friends from before I joined the military, Erin, Jenny, and Kelly, helped me by researching PTSD and gaining an understanding of my disability. It is important for people to know that PTSD can be an actual disability and many victims qualify for assistance. (For more information, please see: http://www.disability-benefits-help.org/disabling-conditions/post-traumatic-stress-disorder-and-social-security-disability.) These friends have allowed me to vent and share with them my struggles without showing pity or making me feel judged.

However, for me, talking to other military sexual trauma (MST) vets is the best way to feel normal. It has been very important to experience validation and to know I am not alone. I was fortunate to be mentored by a wonderful veteran named Wendi Goodman who was a member of the Women's Army Corp and an MST. Wendi told me to consider myself blessed if I have five true close veteran friends who really understand. It took me several years to find that handful, but I now have my battle buddies who always seem to know what to say because they have been there too. They have shown me it is possible to love life again. And finally, in this age of social media, I have met military comrades online who have offered me support and encouragement.

I am grateful to all the people who have helped me along

the way, especially my husband. For me, healing has been a windy path with lots of exits and valleys. But as long as I persevere and keep getting back on the path, I believe I will continue to experience the joys and rewards of recovery.

As we let our own lights shine, we unconsciously give other people permission to do the same. As we are liberated from our own fear, our presence automatically liberates others.

— MARIANNE WILLIAMS

chapter seventeen
TEEN VIOLENCE

ELIINA BELENKIY (eliinabelenkiy.com) *is a graduate student and founder of the organization Regain Your Voice. Eliina has volunteered for many organizations to promote sexual assault awareness and has shared her story with numerous media outlets and submitted testimonies to Congress to help change existing legislation for survivors.*

I am currently a graduate student at George Mason University pursuing a degree in counseling. Sometimes as I leave an evening class, I feel a rush of fear go through my body as I walk to my car. That is because I was raped on a college campus when I was 14 years old by a man I met on the internet. Before we met, I remember him telling me how much he loved me. Later, I came to understand that he was grooming me—chatting online with me several times a day, sometimes for hours. I was raised to be a loving, trusting, and kind individual. Soft-spoken by nature, I was an innocent, vulnerable young teenager who struggled like most adolescents with the realities of life. And I fell victim to a man who lied to me about many things, including his age (he was 40 years old) and who gained my trust.

For years I wondered how I could have let this happen to me, how I could have been so gullible, so naive. For years I blamed myself and felt stuck for the better part of a decade. Trying to regain myself, my voice, and my identity—all of which were lost on that warm summer day, July 10, 2000— has been very difficult, especially since I suffer from PTSD. I used to wake up in the middle of the night, kicking and screaming, trying to push the blankets off of me, feeling as if it was happening all over again.

By the time I testified against my perpetrator in federal court I was getting ready to graduate from high school. The prior three years were just a blur, all spent waiting for my moment on the stand when I would point my finger and identify my attacker. When he was found guilty, I thought that would be the end, but little did I know this was something I would continue to live with every single day.

I met my husband Max when I was 16 years old. We had only been together for a few months, but he came with me the day that I had to testify, held my hand, and reassured me. He also accompanied me to the sentencing and squeezed my hand during the whole hearing. Looking back, it is amazing to me that at such a young age, he knew how to be so supportive and generous, and that he chose to participate in the whole legal process when he had no obligation whatsoever.

Since I was raped on a college campus, I did not have the will to go to college. But Max never gave up hope for my education, gently pushing me for many years to fulfill my potential. He suffers with me through my PTSD symptoms and times of depression. He is also very supportive of my advocacy efforts because he sees that speaking out makes me stronger. Recently, we were in a parking lot at night and I got scared and became very hyper-vigilant. He hugged me and said, "I won't let anything happen to you; you're safe with me." That was exactly what I needed. I do not know where I would be if not for my husband. I had fears after the rape that no one would ever want me, that I was damaged goods, but Max has never once treated me that way.

My mother is another person who was a great source of strength. Sadly, she passed away in 2007, but for those seven years after the assault, she was my biggest ally. She never pushed me to talk about what happened, even though I knew she wanted to know the details. One day, several years after the rape, I did tell her the specifics and she just sat and listened. She didn't start crying or make it about her, but held it together and acted strong for me. I know she felt a lot of guilt as if she should have somehow protected me, but she never projected those feelings onto me. She also helped me with my responsibilities and commitments when I had difficulty keeping up, and she never once pressured me to "get over it" or "move on," so I had the space I needed to grieve, process, and understand what had happened.

Survivors need to be heard, believed, and given patience and kindness. We don't want pity; we just need support and understanding. Intellectually, I know it was not my fault. I know I was groomed by a sexual predator who knew exactly what he was doing, but I came out of it not being able to trust myself or anyone else. It made things worse when friends said insensitive things like, "Shouldn't you be over it by now?" Such comments were hurtful and made me feel as if something was wrong with me. If family and friends would educate themselves on the effects of sexual violence and learn about PTSD, it would be so helpful. Like most survivors, I just want to be listened to without judgment, and I certainly don't want people to avoid me or act afraid to talk about it with me. That only adds to my shame.

My mother used to say, "Everything happens for a reason."

For some victims of sexual assault these words can be very painful, but for me they have been an inspiration. I needed to somehow find a way of turning my experience into something positive. Today, I reach out to survivors on their path to healing and educate others about prevention. I started a photography project and a nonprofit organization called Regain Your Voice. That is the reason I think this happened to me—so I could help others.

There is no greater agony than bearing an untold story inside you.
— MAYA ANGELOU

ELBERETH LUNN CHAHALIS *is a member of the RAINN Speakers'*
Bureau, has volunteered at the Prince George's Hospital Crisis Center, and was
an intern at the International Rescue Committee, working with victims of
human trafficking. Currently, she attends the University of Maryland, Balti-
more, where she is working toward a master's degree in clinical social work.

My nickname is Elby. I am 33 years old, married with two
beautiful daughters, and a graduate student with a dream of
helping people. It wasn't always this way though.

As a teenager, I was a seemingly tough girl who spent all
of her spare time with the wrong crowd. I was drinking and
smoking by the age of thirteen. One rainy night on my way
home I met two guys on the bus who were friendly. I accepted
an invitation to their house party and followed them back to
what turned out to be an abandoned apartment with four
other males waiting in the dark. I was fifteen years old. They
strangled me, beat me, raped me, and left me for dead after
taking my phone number and address with the promise of
more to come should I tell anyone. When I finally gathered
the strength to walk out with my clothes half on, a man
driving by saw me and put me in his car, taking me straight
to the hospital. He did this act of charity anonymously, so I
never got to thank him. As soon as I was in the hospital and
said I was raped, the nurses, police, and staff swept in to care

for me and begin an investigation. All of my predators were caught within two days of my attack, and all but one were charged as adults, found guilty, and are currently serving life sentences without parole.

My greatest friendship came out of my deepest heartache. I attended a teen support group after my attack and met my lifelong confidant, Kristen. She had endured the same shame, guilt, and anger, and we found comfort in each other. More often than not I tried to act tough and not show my real feelings, and even though she could see through my facade, she never called me out on it. She knew it was my way of protecting myself and coping during the first few years after my assault. We had a saying: "I love you, unconditionally," and that was it for us. We have always been there for each other, but we also have allowed space for each other when we needed it.

My brother never attended my trial court hearings or seemed to know much about the assault; if he did, he never said anything. I think he avoided it in the beginning because he was trying to protect me from having to talk about it, but now that we are older I want to share my story with him.

My husband has played a huge role in what I consider my final stages of recovery. I was 22 when we met, finally free from the drugs and alcohol I had used as a method of coping with my pain, and I was looking for a life partner. My spouse comes from a very close-knit family and had never known anyone who had experienced any kind of real hardship.

Initially he struggled significantly with the knowledge of my burden and often became overwhelmed at imagining what I had been through. We both attended a *Take Back the Night* event where I gave my testimony. It was very powerful for me and for him, and I think that is when he started seeing me as a survivor rather than a victim. In the beginning of our relationship, I didn't realize how much I still avoided acting vulnerable, and he made me see how much I was giving up by not being authentic. He has had an enormous impact on my self-image and self-esteem. He is also an incredibly compassionate and wonderful lover.

My mother often still views me as her little girl who was hurt, and more so than not, this bothers me. I have come a long way, and I don't want members of my family to be stuck in the past. Still, except for her occasional mama bear personality, my mother was and is one of my biggest advocates and cheerleaders. I know she feels responsible and guilty for what happened to me, even though it was no more her fault than mine. And yet, I also know she is very proud of who I have become. When I was in the hospital, she was not allowed to hug me or hold my hand or stroke my hair, because every inch of my body was evidence. That was difficult for all of us, but it also brought us back together as a family. In some ways my attack was like an intervention on my life. My family stood beside me in court, and my mom wrote a powerful victim impact statement which she read at the sentencing.

The one thing that some family members have been unable or unwilling to help me with is attending *Take Back the Night* events. It has become an annual ritual for me, allowing me time to mourn and commemorate with other survivors. I realize to some outsiders this may seem like an evening of wallowing in sadness, but it is so much more than that. Seeing men, women, children, and grandparents all come together and unveil their mask of anonymity is incredibly powerful, both to a fellow survivor and to those visiting. I heard a story about a teenage boy who had attended the event and a year later, he intervened when a girl was at risk of assault at a local party. Because of *Take Back the Night*, he was able to have a life-changing impact on that girl.

The Akan people of Ghana have a saying about taking from the past what is good and bringing it into the present in order to make positive progress through the benevolent use of knowledge:

Se wo were fi na wosankofa a yenkyi,
It is not wrong to go back for that which you have forgotten.

QUASONA COBB (quasonacobb.com) *is a New York City native working for a Fortune 150 company. An advocate for the prevention of dating violence, Quasona shares her story at churches, local agencies, and educational institutions including the Children's Aid Society and the Administration for Children's Services. She has been featured in Glamour Magazine and was a guest on Katie Couric's talk show.*

I am a teen-dating violence survivor. Beginning at the age of 17 until I was 21 years old, I was in a destructive relationship with a man five years older than me. In the beginning he was wonderful—charming, handsome, and fun to be around. But after almost a year together, he began to verbally abuse me and then he started hitting me and raping me. We were living together by then and like other victims of domestic abuse, I developed a false sense of control over my abuser's violent outbursts. I thought that if I could keep quiet and do whatever he asked during the arguments, I wouldn't feel his wrath. Of course, it never worked; I had no control over him or his actions. To him I was property.

I kept the abuse a secret for such a long time. I stayed away from family and friends when my bruises were visible. And when I did see anyone, I mustered up a smile and pretended I was okay even though I was hurting inside. I come from a family of such strong women, so whenever I was around them, I put on my best tough-girl impression. I was embarrassed by the thought of telling them what was going on. When people ask me what the warning signs of domestic abuse are, I tell them isolation is the biggest.

The last night that I was with my abusive ex, he threatened my life. The next morning I had my locks changed and packed a bag of clothes and headed to my grandparents' house to break my years of silence. Shortly after, my ex-boyfriend met up with my mother to clear his belongings from my apartment. That day he brutally assaulted my poor mother to the point that she had to be hospitalized.

I was an absolute wreck while my mother was in the hospital and felt riddled with guilt and anger. My immediate family stepped up during my mother's recovery. I pressed charges, and they were all very supportive of the court process (which ended in a conviction and prison sentence), but I do not think they really understood the magnitude of the abuse that I suffered. Sometimes I wonder if they blame me for what happened to my mom because I was the one involved with this person. I don't think it's fair to ever blame the victim, regardless of the circumstances.

In high school I had a very strong circle of friends, but after the conviction, it dwindled down to an occasional "hello" text message. I think the situation was too much for them and they wanted to distance themselves from me. I was really disappointed, sometimes angry, but I let go of that hurt because I needed to heal.

I ended up building a strong friendship with an amazing girl named Bianca Velez. Bianca had gone to the same high school I did, but we did not know each other very well. She showed me compassion, and I gravitated toward her sisterly love. I remember calling her crying one night while she was out celebrating another friend's birthday. Though she was at a party, she took the time to comfort and reassure me. Whenever I need a friend and an ally, Bianca is there. From time to time I send her little thank you notes, and she always replies with something like, "You know I would never let you go through this alone!" "I love you and I'm proud of you," or "I know how hard it is to let others in; thank you for letting me be there for you." It's people like Bianca who survivors need during the healing process. She never judges me, and I will always be grateful for her unwavering support.

Before all of this happened, I was a very positive person. But afterwards, I was extremely jumpy and easily startled. Sometimes I would shriek with anxiety, and I remember someone in my family saying it was "annoying and childlike." I was very hurt by the dismissal, like I was wrong for what I was going through. In therapy I learned that I was experiencing symptoms of PTSD. I wish my family and friends understood that four years of trauma do not just vanish when the assaulter is incarcerated.

I am now 26 years old and have entered a new relationship and continue to create new friendships in hopes of rebuilding my life. It is very hard to trust someone and to become intimate after suffering dating violence, but I knew I shouldn't generalize about everyone based on one horrible experience. Cautious not to repeat bad dating habits, I almost immediately got my family involved in my new relationship. My current boyfriend and I began just hanging out, and I was very upfront about the things I was going through. I believe it has been a learning experience for both of us. As my mother's condition improved, she asked to meet my new boyfriend. I was nervous, but I knew her stamp of approval was needed for me to continue the relationship. I am most grateful for his friendship. He is full of patience, support, love, and optimism; those are very contagious characteristics.

Because I have undergone so much healing, I am now able to be an advocate for the prevention of dating violence. Speaking out publicly about my experience has been the hardest thing that I have ever done, but it has taught me so much about myself. I no longer blame myself or feel ashamed, and when I am triggered, I am not afraid to ask for help. Survivors have the right to grieve, to be scared, and to be angry; those are all parts of the recovery process. It is important that we lovingly give ourselves time to heal. Yet even with healing, we and others must recognize that because of the abuse, our lives have been forever changed.

Freeing yourself was one thing;
claiming ownership of that freed self was another.

— TONI MORRISON

chapter eighteen
IN OUR SCHOOLS

ANTHONY ANDRES is co-founder of the 12 After 12 Empowerment and Asset of Character 12 Step Program. He has written for the SESAME (Stop Educator Sexual Abuse, Misconduct and Exploitation) website, and is currently in school pursuing his dream to be a licensed alcohol and drug counselor.

The abuse I suffered started when I was in the eighth grade. The teacher we had that year was new, and all the kids thought he was cool. He right away took a liking to me, which boosted my self-esteem and outlook on life. Towards the end of the school year he even helped me get a job by hiring me at a coffee shop he had opened with a few of his friends. He also invited me to stay the night at his house after work. My mom thought it was a little strange to be spending this much time with my teacher, but I told her everything was okay and that it was convenient because we would both be going to school in the morning. At the time, it was okay, but looking back I realize making me feel safe was part of my abuser's plan. He was grooming me.

Once junior high graduation was over and he was not my

teacher anymore, he initiated sexual contact with me. I was horrified. I didn't want to do it, but I didn't know how to say no. Here I thought he was my best friend and now he was my employer. Worst of all, I had told everyone in my life that he was a good guy, yet the dangers my family had tried to warn me about were coming true. He also gave me drugs and alcohol, and this is when my addictions took off. Not only did I have the genetic predisposition for chemical dependency, but I constantly felt shame and fear which I wanted desperately to escape. The drugs and alcohol offered me that escape. As I began to lose the ability to face my life, my addiction worsened, drawing me back to my abuser's house. This awful cycle continued for three years.

When I was 21, I finally broke the silence. Immediately, my father told me that he loved me no matter what, and then my mother shared about the abuse she had endured as a child. She had gone through a similar experience and vowed never to let anything like this happen to me. The abuse in her life was one of the contributing factors for her descent into chemical dependency, and now she was painfully witnessing this cycle all over again in my life.

A few months later we went to trial. Both my parents and I testified only to have my abuser acquitted on all counts because of the way the charges were brought and the burden of proof we had to meet. This made national news. It was an awful time in my life, and I felt as if I was being victimized all over again.

Over the next few years I spiraled further and further into an abyss of drug abuse accompanied by suicidal feelings. I was tormented by self-hatred, pain, and confusion. I didn't feel like I could handle life as other people and suffered in and out of treatments and psych wards. But through it all, they were there, my wonderful mom and dad. They never gave up hope that I would someday recover. My parents brought me to group therapies and helped me share about the abuse during family week in treatment. Finally, their efforts paid off, and at the age of 26, I found sobriety and began to heal.

For me, recovery has been an act of courage, a decision to face life as it is, and a test of faith that somehow I could reclaim my dignity. I know there are many people who have endured hardships like these, but in order to face my own, I had to rely on the experience of others who had suffered in a similar manner. Group support is a great help to survivors. To be able to walk together and share hope with one another fortifies us and helps us realize we are not alone. Through our combined stories we are empowered to make changes in our own lives, and inspired to do whatever we can to prevent these terrible things from happening to others.

If I have one message for parents it would be to know where your kids are, with whom they are associating, and what exactly they are doing. See with your own eyes, and don't take your kids' words at face value. My parents checked up on me from time to time, and I know they tried to do the best they could with the information I provided them. However, because the abuse was something I was so ashamed of, I kept it a secret and they didn't know how to break through that secrecy. I don't blame them, but I do want to make others aware of these dangers. Further and persistent investigation on the part of parents could intimidate and stop someone who has nefarious intentions.

Today, my mom and dad get to look into the eyes of their emotionally beautiful and resilient son. And because my mom and dad gave me the strength to heal, I have been able to help them heal from the sorrow and guilt they felt for not being able to protect me. We have all made amazing transformations,

and together we offer our experience in the two-fold hope
that it will help others and raise awareness about the prevalence and devastation of sexual abuse.

When we are no longer able to change a situation,
we are challenged to change ourselves.

—VIKTOR E. FRANKL

NIKKI WILLIAMS is the creator of "Raising Healthy Athletes," devoted to educating those who work in youth athletics about the dangers of blurred boundaries and how to protect young athletes from abuse. She is also a PIAA track and field official, a board member of Joshua Development Corporation, and the proud mother of two adult sons.

When I was growing up, track and field was my whole life! I ran track from fifth grade through twelfth grade (1982-1990) with the same coach. By the time I was in middle school I was running year-round. It was my track coach who sexually abused me.

Many years later when I was able to confront the abuse, I made inquiries about this coach and found out he was still working at the all-girls Catholic high school where I graduated. I had a meeting with the Catholic Bishop who oversaw the school and told him my story. After consulting with his attorney, they immediately met with my perpetrator and released him of his coaching duties. I wanted to press charges, but after an investigation from the D.A.'s office, I was told that the statute of limitation had expired for criminal court. I was devastated, but at least I knew he was unable to hurt more children at the school I attended.

The road was long and difficult that took me to a place of being able to work through what happened to me. Though

I exhibited many symptoms of post-traumatic stress disorder, I had repressed all memories of the abuse until I was 36 years old. I could never understand why I was suffering or acting out in unhealthy ways. I had to drop out of college because I had significant problems with concentration, and at an early age I was in an abusive marriage even though my parents had been wonderful role models. For years, I found it nearly impossible to trust people.

It was in October of 2008 that things began to unravel. The last thing I remember was walking into an elevator with my dear friend Tim. Then two days later, I was being comforted by my parents at their home in Erie, Pennsylvania. I had no memory of jumping out of Tim's moving car, or of being examined in the emergency room, or of then being taken to my parents' home to recover. It took a week for my memory to return. It was very frightening, and when I was strong enough, I decided to go back to my own home in Pittsburgh to see a neurologist and find out what was wrong with me. After lots of testing the neurologist diagnosed me with transient global amnesia. According to Mayo Clinic, "Transient global amnesia is a sudden, temporary episode of memory loss that can't be attributed to a more common neurological condition." Soon after, I was diagnosed with PTSD by a psychiatrist.

One night I was sitting with Tim and he simply asked, "What happened to you Nikki?" Without missing a beat I spoke the words, "My coach raped me." I then broke down sobbing in his arms, feeling both shocked and relieved. Immediately the flashbacks started, and over time I became flooded with memories. I know it can be hard for people to understand repression or how painful the return of memories can be. I also know the abuse I suffered was a very real thing and stole much of my life from me.

Soon after I went back to my parents' house and told them and one of my siblings about the abuse. They were amazingly supportive. We all cried and hugged each other and vowed that we would make it through to the other side. My parents told me that they would support me in whatever ways I needed them to. This was a huge gift to me and one I wish all survivors could receive.

I was very, very fortunate to be able to take a leave of absence from work. I signed myself into an intensive outpatient rehabilitation program at a local psychiatric hospital, where I attended group therapy three days a week and visited with a psychiatrist weekly. After completing the program I continued weekly counseling at my local rape crisis center. It was there I found the courage to rebuild my life.

My parents have always been my biggest supporters. They never asked me questions about the abuse itself; instead they tenderly offered support and loving advice. They let me lead and trusted my timing, judgment, and space. They acknowledged my inner strength and reminded me of who I am as a person and who I was created to be. From all of this, they showed me that I possessed within myself everything I needed to heal. And yet, the most powerful thing they did was simply to hug me. As small as a hug can be, it is a huge thing for a survivor in pain. Tim too has been a great support to me, constantly reassuring me of my bravery and always being there if I need him. My faith has also been a huge help to me.

I decided I wanted to do something to help others in athletics, so one evening I grabbed my laptop and created two powerful training sessions to empower young athletes and their parents and educate them about the athlete/coach relationship. It was almost as if my warrior spirit kicked in and this was my way of fighting back. Since then I have also created a session for coaches to train them on appropriate boundaries, how and when to blow the whistle on colleagues who have clearly overstepped their boundaries, and the effects of childhood abuse on victims, families, communities, and ultimately our world.

Today I am living a satisfied life. However, there will always be a hole in my heart as a result of what my coach did to me. I know there are so many other victims out there hurting, so I try to be a voice for the voiceless and a face to those victims who are afraid to show theirs.

I learned that courage was not the absence of fear
but the triumph over it.

— NELSON MANDELA

chapter nineteen

MULTIPLE PERPETRATORS

JARROD NOFTSGER *is a faculty member at Oklahoma State University. He advocates awareness of domestic violence, sexual assault, and child safety. Jarrod has appeared on numerous TV and radio programs, including "The Oprah Winfrey Show," NPR's "On Point with Tom Ashbrook," and "The Huffington Post, Live with Josh Zepps."*

Most of my adult life was an uneasy truce between two selves: the desperate boy demanding to be heard and the demanding man desperate for silence. Beginning at the age of eight until I was eleven, I was abused by a best friend and his older brother. At eight years old, the paradox of longing for help and yet panicked that anyone would find out governed my thoughts and actions. I was deeply troubled by a number of terrible things that I imagined would happen if my secret was revealed. I was fearful that my friends would make fun of me. I was scared that I was going to be in trouble for "what I had done." I was angry that I was unable to stop the abuse. Most of all, I was terrified that my parents would no longer love me.

A year later, at the age of twelve, I was targeted and

groomed by a youth group sponsor from the Episcopal Church my family and I attended. Sadly, the experience of serial abuse is not uncommon among children, as perpetrators often have an uncanny ability to find young people who have been previously victimized.

For a boy abused by a male, it is typical for the boy to be confused about his sexuality. Biologically there may have been pleasure from the abuse; at the same time the boy may have been terrified by what was happening. This confusion can be compounded if the abuser told the boy that he clearly wanted what occurred or he would not have had an erection. If the boy is not gay, the confusion caused can create feelings of uncertainty that can complicate intimacy throughout life. If the boy is gay, he may worry that he somehow attracted the abuse through some unknown signal. Either scenario creates a burden of doubt and shame that often locks boys into a life of silence.

The trauma I suffered as a child came to define my identity and shape my interactions with the world. For over 30 years I suffered in silence—an overachiever searching for strength through my learned definition of masculinity. However, in my early forties, I went from never thinking about the abuse to being tormented by it at every turn. In time I would find the answer to why. Most significantly, my children had reached the age that I was when I was first abused. Secondly, I was successful and productive in my career. Likewise, I was at a strong place in my marriage where I felt safe and secure. My brain had the set of perfect conditions needed for me to confront what I had long suppressed. And so began my journey to find peace with who I am as a man, as a father, and as a husband.

I first told my story to a group of men in an anonymous support group. It was there that I awkwardly began to confront what had been done to me. These brave men gave me the courage to tell my wife the full story. With the guidance of a qualified therapist, I would also tell my children, extended family, and my closest friends. This gradual telling and retelling of my story began a remarkable process of shedding the shame and fear that bound me. I would later go on to tell my story to groups of people, including the media. Every word I spoke validated what was for so long hidden. Equally important, speaking the truth to others gave them the courage to confront their own childhood traumas. The idea of taking something so dreadful and using it for healing remains a very powerful tool in my own journey.

Though our lives were turned upside down, from the start, my wife made it clear to me daily that she was committed to our marriage. An interesting aside is that two weeks before we married, through trembling and tears, I summoned every ounce of courage available and told her my secret: "Before we met, I was involved in a same-sex relationship." "Wait! What?" After answering her questions, she adamantly pointed out, "That is not a relationship; it is child abuse." But I continued to believe it was my fault and having done the honorable thing by telling her, I proceeded to successfully push the trauma as far away from my consciousness as possible.

When I told my children, they were also supportive and brave even when their friends at school asked questions such as, "Why didn't your dad fight back?" By this time, I had gone public. It is staggering to me what is possible when there is trust and authenticity among loved ones. The sheer weight that was lifted from no longer carrying around the secret made me a more present father and husband and improved our relationships in ways I could never have imagined.

There have been many others who have stood beside me. There is my older brother who expressed sadness that he was not aware and that he did not keep me safe. There is the friend who did not know what to say other than, "I am sorry that happened to you." My boss also played a key role, being patient with requested time off for therapy appointments and on those days when I simply needed to retreat home, too overwhelmed to function at my full potential.

Advice for those wanting to help: love, listen, believe, and accept the impact the abuse has had on the survivor's life. Very likely, the survivor will first need to come to terms with himself and perhaps even forgive himself for what happened. The process can be tumultuous, but as he does this, he will be able to love more deeply, trust more fully, and experience life more richly.

Fortunately, I achieved these things. My story has a happy ending. I no longer see the abuse as the defining characteristic of my identity, but rather as only one significant part of my life journey.

The real voyage of discovery consists not in seeking new landscapes, but in having new eyes.

—MARCEL PROUST

CHRISTINE "CISSY" WHITE *is a break-the-cycle mother who has been widely published in the Boston Globe, Ms. Magazine, Elephant Journal, and Spirituality & Health magazine. As the founder of the Heal Write Now Center, she leads writing workshops, gives presentations, and helps nonprofits understand and discover creative solutions for traumatic stress. Find her at healwritenow.com.*

There are times I awake so numb from a nightmare I feel like an iceberg. It's hard for me to cry when I feel terror. Symptoms of PTSD are how the past arrives in the middle of my present without my permission. For me it's physical, and luckily, it always passes. People know that fireworks can cause flashbacks for veterans. For those of us who were abused as children, there are many firecrackers.

Calm, tactile comfort helps. A shower, taking breaths, doing yoga, and smelling something nice are all things that ground me. Most important is the feeling that someone genuinely cares and isn't burdened by my symptoms. Thankfully I have a few such people in my life. When the symptoms fade into the background, I can enjoy the life I have worked hard to create. I have a beautiful daughter. We live in a cottage by the ocean. My friends and loved ones are loyal and inspiring. My ex and I have a strong relationship and have done recovery work individually and together in order to co-parent well.

My work is creative and my bills are paid. I've dated, and finally, after many years and much bodywork, I am able to enjoy sex.

Like many victims, the abuse defined my youth. My stepfather was 45 when he married my 19-year-old mother. I was sexually molested by him and two of his children—one male and one female—intermittently throughout my childhood. Unlike my stepfather and stepbrother, my stepsister was often nice to me, and so her abuse was the most confusing of the three. The scars are deep and I still sometimes sleep face down, arms under me, and legs crossed. But in contrast to when I was little, I can now remind myself that I am safe; I can stretch and breathe and listen to guided imagery or calming music.

I wish with all my heart my mother had protected me, but in the early days, she did not even believe me. In her defense, my stepfather preyed on her vulnerability. She was so young and had escaped her own traumatic childhood and an abusive teen marriage, and she was poor. However, even now my mother has difficulty giving me the love and support I will always crave.

Luckily, my Aunt Worry did believe me. She opened her heart and her home and was loyal and loving, especially during my teens and twenties. She not only helped me, but also allowed me to help her in return. I learned that family relationships could be reciprocal, positive, and even fun.

My friend Kathy has also been a huge source of support, in part, because she is not a survivor herself. It has been helpful to learn about life from her perspective. I have discovered that certain things I thought were related to the abuse are just normal emotions and problems that all people struggle with, and that has been a great relief to me. Conversely, this same friend extends unlimited praise for the ways I mother my daughter, knowing that I didn't receive role modeling, and she encourages me to reframe self-hatred so that I think of myself as a brave warrior/learner when I am tempted to feel stupid or damaged.

In addition, my neighbor, who I call Nana Connie, sees me in a softer, more loving light than I often see myself. She thinks I'm fun, smart, and strong and tells me so, expressing an unconditional maternal love that has been wonderful to experience as an adult.

And so you see, I've been healed by the kindness, gentleness, and concern of those not afraid of my pain and who do not try to fix me—something which would only make me feel worse. In my advocacy work, I have met many survivors, and I think what we all seek is a simple hug, a showing up at the door with flowers or soup, and someone to say, "I love you, and I'm so sorry for what happened to you."

Along with the support of these loving people, writing has been enormously important to my recovery. It helped me as a child, and it has helped me throughout my entire adult life. Often, survivors may need to learn better ways to self-soothe, to express and find relief from trauma symptoms. In the workshops I lead, I have come to believe that writing is one of our most powerful tools in learning to do these things. Writing can help to liberate us from the pain and shame we feel. My website, healwritenow.com, may prove useful in this pursuit.

It's grueling work to break the cycle of abuse and neglect and become a healthy, whole person. Still, I truly believe that though we cannot change the past we absolutely can create a better present and future, no matter what we have suffered. The rewards for healing are many, not just for us but for those we love. My greatest successes are when my daughter laughs or the times when I feel broken and practice self-love and self-acceptance. Once, my daughter handed me her fleece blanket and said, "It needs to be recharged with mama love." I wore it all day and gave it back to her that night. And whenever I tell her I love her, she invariably says, "I know." I have broken the cycle. Parenting. Love. Intimacy. There were years I doubted any of these were possible for me, yet here I am today experiencing them all.

It takes two to speak truth, one to speak and another to hear.
— HENRY DAVID THOREAU

MICHAEL SKINNER (mskinnermusic.com) *is an award-winning advocate, educator, writer, and musician. The founder and director of the nonprofit "Surviving Spirit," he has appeared on "The Oprah Winfrey Show" and been a presenter at The National Press Club and at The United Nations, State Department, and Georgetown University Conference on Sexual Exploitation and Trafficking.*

I'm a father, grandfather, and friend. Professionally, I'm a musician who plays the guitar, sings, writes songs, plays the drums, and has released three albums. I'm also an advocate, public speaker, and writer of published articles that address the concerns of mental health, trauma, and abuse.

Who I am as a person is very important to me because for many years of my life all I felt was shame, fear, and disgust. Despite any accomplishments I achieved as a musician, father, husband, and business owner, I lived with a deep hole in my soul that no amount of effort or trying to be good was able to fill.

The cause of my unremitting pain and self-hatred is that I experienced brutal and sadistic sexual abuse by both of my parents beginning when I was a very young child and continuing into my mid-teens. What made the abuse even more damaging for me was the participation of other equally perverted adults who were friends of my parents—a biker, an ex-cop who had been thrown off the force, heavy drinkers—both male and female.

For a long time, I tried desperately to rid my mind of these horrors, but I was unable to do so, and the images of my past were a constant reminder of the dirtiness I felt. It was more than I could handle alone and yet the taboo of talking about sexual abuse led me to isolation. As an adult, I was diagnosed with both post-traumatic stress disorder and depression and was called "mentally ill." There was a lot of blame, shame, and telling me to "just get over it." All of this severely impacted my ability to heal, making it difficult to navigate my way into a better future. But navigate I did. And like other survivors, I did not do it alone.

Though my recovery has been long and difficult, the rewards have been many. The very things that helped me in my youth—music and being in nature—have given me a new lease on life. I have also learned how to surround myself with loving people. Especially wonderful has been the acceptance and understanding of my friend Mary. Her love and encouragement did wonders for building my self-esteem. She encouraged me to perform again as a drummer. Gaining the confidence to return to my music and do what I love has been immensely therapeutic. When people are neither afraid nor blame me for the intrusive feelings and thoughts of the past, it is a gift. Friends and family need to realize that even one person's love and support can make a world of difference. I no longer feel weak or ashamed; I feel valued and cherished. I am finally free of the negative assumptions people once imposed upon me, and I now honor the courage, perseverance, and resiliency I had as a young boy to survive the terrors of my youth.   Another thing that has been healing for me is to learn all I could about trauma and abuse and how it can cause physiological changes in those of us who have been sexually victimized. There is much research showing how sexual abuse affects the brain and nervous system development, and that the younger the victim is when the abuse begins, the more harm it generally causes. Researching the ramifications of abuse can be very empowering for survivors and I encourage both them and those who love them to find out as much as they can. Dr. Bessel van der Kolk's work is a good place to begin. A former president of the International Society for Traumatic Stress Studies and a professor of psychiatry at Boston University School of Medicine, Dr. van der Kolk has published extensively on the effects trauma can have on development.

Survivors cannot heal in isolation. The shame and blame festers when we are left alone. We need to know we can thrive despite what happened in the past. And that thriving is enormously nourished and enriched when we are supported and accepted by others. Receiving compassion and love do wonders for all of us. Someday, I hope there will be a worldwide campaign to make people aware of the lifetime consequences that result from sexual abuse. I am attempting to do my small part in facilitating that awareness. I try my best to live each day to the fullest and show by example that it is possible to overcome trauma, no matter how horrific. I do a lot of advocacy work, and helping others helps me. Whatever I give, I always get back more. Lastly, I practice mindfulness and this gives balance to my life. I work, I play, and I rest. Dr. Jim Hopper's work on "Mindfulness and Kindness" is another great resource.

Recovery is a slow process, and the truth is I doubt that I'll ever fully recover from what happened to me. But that's okay because I believe I am a better man for the suffering I've endured. All I ever wanted as a child was to love, be loved, and live without fear. Though it has taken me a long time to get to a place where these things are a reality in my life, I am deeply grateful that I have finally arrived.

You cannot heal what you do not acknowledge,
and what you do not consciously acknowledge will remain
in control of you from within,
festering and destroying you and those around you.

— RICHARD ROHR

chapter twenty
FINAL WORDS / FINAL TIPS

On behalf of myself, the nineteen survivor contributors, and victims everywhere, I wish to thank you for taking the time to read this book. I hope you have gained an understanding as to why social support is so crucial to recovery. I also hope you have come to realize that whenever light is shed on a topic, darkness and pain are diminished. And most of all, I hope you have been personally inspired and empowered to take an active role in the healing process of a loved one who has been sexually victimized.

If you seek further guidance, my website, youcanhelp-survivors.com, contains resources and blogs that may prove useful. On it you will find "Five Ways to Help Your Loved One Heal," which I now include in this last chapter. These five ways are essentially a brief and very incomplete summary of all that has been shared in Parts One and Two. However, if you become overwhelmed and start to lose your way, these five and final tips may provide clarity and act as a compass.

(1) **REASSURE**. Victims of sexual abuse and assault generally suffer from deep and pervasive feelings of shame. What has happened to them is a violation not just of the body but also

of the spirit, often resulting in low self-esteem and a loss of dignity. Tell your loved one that you (a) believe, (b) respect, (c) love, and (d) admire her or him. Reassuring words are powerful healing tools.

(2) **LISTEN**. Perhaps the most important and effective thing you can do to facilitate the healing of someone who has been sexually abused or assaulted is to encourage that person to talk about his or her trauma and then to listen with your heart. Because of the sheer ugliness of the events, many well-intentioned people choose silence over open communication. Silence is the biggest obstacle to recovery.

(3) **LEARN**. There are many resources that inform and educate family and friends as to the symptoms and effects of sexual trauma. Be proactive. If your loved one suffers from PTSD, learning about the disorder will enable you to understand and comfort your loved one during those painful times. Another way to learn how you can help is to simply and lovingly ask, "What can I do?"

(4) **SUPPORT**. Support your loved one by acknowledging the courage and tenacity it takes to work through the trauma. That work nearly always includes therapy and/or group counseling. Sometimes it involves going back to school or changing careers. If you are in a position to assist financially and your loved one cannot afford these things, providing that support is a wise investment.

(5) **CELEBRATE**. It is a highly rewarding albeit difficult endeavor to participate in the healing of a loved one. Celebrate the achievements! Even when old behaviors and debilitating symptoms reappear, do not let those negate the progress that

has been made. Believe in your loved one's ability to create a healthy life, and whenever and however possible, provide outlets that bring levity and joy.

What if we take our broken dreams
you and I
and recycle them?
Plant them as seeds in
the gardens of our hearts
and wait till harvest time
when death gives way to life?
Or throw them to the wind
and watch them ride on birds' wings
closer to the sun than our dark nights
could ever have imagined?
Or put them into our hot baths
and let the saltiness from our tears
soften our skins to silk?
Why there must be a trillion ways
to turn misfortunes and mistakes into magic.

— REBECCA STREET

ACKNOWLEDGEMENTS

I want to thank the numerous brave women and men who participated in my research, sharing their struggles and strengths—all with the goal of helping others. Particularly inspiring to me have been the nineteen remarkable survivors whose stories appear in *You Can Help*. Each of them enriched my life and my work.

A special thank you to Mike Lew, author of *Victims No Longer*, who championed my efforts from the very beginning and who gave my vision credibility. Also noteworthy are RAINN (The Rape, Abuse, and Incest National Network), Dr. David Lisak of the Bristlecone Project, David Clohessy of SNAP (Survivors Network of those Abused by Priests), and Protect Our Defenders. They all encouraged my writing and kindly assisted me in recruiting the wide range of survivors required to give the book balance.

Most of all, I want to thank my wonderful family—my children, Abbot and Amanda Street, and my brothers, John, Jim, and Tom Beers—who have provided light in times of darkness and whose love has made all the difference. I am grateful for their support in the writing of this very personal book, and for my brother John's invaluable business advice.

And to my treasured friends, past and present, who understand that secrets only keep us sick: you have aided me more than you know on my journey to wholeness.

Finally, I want to thank my daughter-in-law, Beth Street, who was my extraordinary editor and faithful cheerleader, and my son-in-law, Jason Bacasa, who beautifully designed my book and website and graciously held my hand throughout the publishing process.

NOTES

1. "Child Sexual Abuse Fact Sheet," The National Child Traumatic Stress Network, 2009: 3, http://nctsn.org/nctsn_assets/pdfs/caring/ChildSexualAbuseFactSheet.pdf.

2. "Statistics About Sexual Violence," National Sexual Violence Resource Center, 2015: 1, http://www.nsvrc.org/sites/default/files/publications_nsvrc_factsheet_media-packet_statistics-about-sexual-violence_0.pdf.

3. Jim Hopper, "Recovered Memories of Sexual Abuse: Scientific Research and Scholarly Resources," modified January 22, 2015, www.jimhopper.com/memory/.

4. "Victims of Sexual Violence: Statistics," Rape, Abuse, and Incest National Network, accessed January 12, 2014, https://rainn.org/statistics/victims-sexual-violence.

5. National Center for Victims of Crime, "Rape-Related Posttraumatic Stress Disorder," *New York City Alliance Against Sexual Assault*, 1992, accessed December 3, 2015, http://www.svfreenyc.org/survivors_factsheet_43.html.

6. Dean G. Kilpatrick, "The Mental Health Impact of Rape," National Violence Against Women Prevention Research Center, Medical University of South Carolina, 2000, https://mainweb-v.musc.edu/vawprevention/

research/mentalimpact.shtml.

7. Susanne Babbel, "Trauma: Childhood Sexual Abuse," *Psychology Today*, March 12, 2013, https://www.psychologytoday.com/blog/somatic-psychology/201303/trauma-childhood-sexual-abuse.

8. U.S. Department of Justice, "Facts and Statistics: Disclosure Among Victims," National Sex Offender Public Registry Website, accessed March 23, 2016,
https://www.nsopw.gov/en-US/Education/FactsStatistics.

9. Judith Lewis Herman, *Trauma and Recovery* (New York: Basic Books, 1997).

10. Dan Gottlieb, "Healing is Feeling Compassion for your Own Trauma," "On Healing" (column in *Philadelphia Inquirer*,) September 1, 2003, http://www.drdangottlieb.com/2003/09/01/on-healing-912003-healing-is-feeling-compassion-for-your-own-trauma/#prettyPhoto.

11. Julia M. Whealin, "Men and Sexual Trauma," New York City Alliance Against Sexual Assault, accessed December 2014, http://www.svfreenyc.org/survivors_factsheet_96.html.

12. National Center for Victims of Crime, "Rape-Related Posttraumatic Stress Disorder," New York City Alliance Against Sexual Assault, 1992, accessed December 3, 2015, http://www.svfreenyc.org/survivors_factsheet_43.html.

13. Cathy Spatz Widom and Michael G. Maxfield, "An Update on the 'Cycle of Violence,'" National Criminal Justice Reference Service, 2001, https://www.ncjrs.gov/txtfiles1/nij/184894.txt.

14. Judith Thompson, "Reflections on Compassion and Social Healing: An Interview with Judith Thompson," Boston Research Center, September 2002, http://www.ikedacenter.org/thinkers-themes/themes/restorative-justice/thompson-compassion-social-healing.

15. "Post-Traumatic Stress Disorder: Definition," *Psychology Today*, modified November 18, 2015, https://www.psychologytoday.com/conditions/post-traumatic-stress-disorder.

16. "PTSD: A Growing Epidemic," *National Institute of Health Medline Plus*, Winter 2009 Issue: Volume 4 Number 1, https://www.nlm.nih.gov/medlineplus/magazine/issues/winter09/articles/winter09pg10-14.html.

17. National Center for Victims of Crime, "Rape-Related Posttraumatic Stress Disorder," New York City Alliance Against Sexual Assault, 1992, accessed December 3, 2015, http://www.svfreenyc.org/survivors_factsheet_43.html.

18. "How Common is PTSD?" National Center for PTSD, modified August 13, 2015, http://www.ptsd.va.gov/public/PTSD-overview/basics/how-common-is-ptsd.asp.

19. "Post-Traumatic Stress Disorder: Symptoms," *U.S. National Library of Medicine Medical Encyclopedia*, modified June 7, 2016, https://www.nlm.nih.gov/medlineplus/ency/article/000925.htm.

20. "Complex PTSD," National Center for PTSD, modified February 23, 2016, http://www.ptsd.va.gov/professional/PTSD-overview/complex-ptsd.asp.

21. "Post-Traumatic Stress Disorder: Definition," *Psychology Today*, modified November 18, 2015, https://www.psychologytoday.com/conditions/post-traumatic-stress-disorder.

22. Alan Wolfelt, "Helping Someone Who Is Grieving," Center for Loss & Life Transition, accessed May 24, 2016, https://www.centerforloss.com/grief/help-someone-grieving/.

23. "Rape in America: A Report to the Nation," National Victim Center

and Crime Victims Research and Treatment Center, April 23, 1992: 7, https://www.musc.edu/ncvc/resources_prof/rape_in_america.pdf.

24. Ken Read-Brown, "Norman Cousins: Editor and Writer (Unitarian Friend), 1915-1990," Harvard Square Library, http://www.harvardsquarelibrary.org/biographies/norman-cousins-2/.

25. Richard B. Gartner, "Talking About Sexually Abused Boys and the Men They Become," *Psychology Today*, January 30, 2011, http://www.psychologytoday.com/blog/psychoanalysis-30/201101/talking-about-sexually-abused-boys-and-the-men-they-become.

26. Sharon Otterman and Ray Rivera, "Ultra-Orthodox Shun Their Own for Reporting Child Sexual Abuse," *New York Times*, May 9, 2012, http://www.nytimes.com/2012/05/10/nyregion/ultra-orthodox-jews-shun-their-own-for-reporting-child-sexual-abuse.html?pagewanted=all&_r=0.

27. Saroj Pathirana, "Sri Lanka's Hidden Scourge of Religious Child Abuse," BBC, June 1, 2012, http://www.bbc.com/news/world-south-asia-15507304.

28. "Dissociative Disorders: Overview," National Alliance on Mental Health, accessed August 12, 2015, http://www.nami.org/Learn-More/Mental-Health-Conditions/Dissociative-Disorders/Overview.

29. Jim Hopper, "Recovered Memories of Sexual Abuse: Scientific Research and Scholarly Resources," modified January 22, 2015, www.jimhopper.com/memory/.

30. "What Is a Dissociative Disorder?" Sidran Institute, accessed October 29, 2015, http://www.sidran.org/resources/for-survivors-and-loved-ones/what-is-a-dissociative-disorder/.

31. Jose R. Maldonado and David Spiegel, "Dissociative Disorders," in *The American Psychiatric Publishing: Board Review Guide for Psychiatry*, ed. James Bourgeios (Arlington: American Psychiatric Pub., 2009), 399.

32. Lisa Trei, "Psychologists offer proof of brain's ability to suppress memories," *Stanford Report*, January 8, 2004, http://news.stanford.edu/news/2004/january14/memory-114.html.

33. *Merriam-Webster's Collegiate Dictionary*, 11th ed., s.v. "shame."

34. *Oxford Dictionaries*, s.v. "shame," accessed April 11, 2016, http://www.oxforddictionaries.com/us/definition/american_english/shame.

35. Judith Lewis Herman, "PTSD as a Shame Disorder," Cambridge Health Alliance, March 10, 2007: 4-6, http://www.challiance.org/Resource.ashx?sn=VOVShattered20ShameJHerman.

36. Brene Brown, "Listening to Shame," TED, https://www.ted.com/talks/brene_brown_listening_to_shame?language=en.

ABOUT THE AUTHOR

REBECCA STREET is an actor, mother of two, and grandmother. She is also a survivor of childhood sexual abuse.

She began her acting career at the Arena Stage in Washington, DC and has performed extensively in Los Angeles and New York in TV, film, and theater. Prior to becoming an actor, she was a public high school English teacher in Maryland where she received a Rotary Club Outstanding Teacher award.

A social activist, she began volunteer work at the age of eleven at the Little Sisters of the Poor Home for the Aged in DC. Through the years, she has taught at a wide variety of nonprofits addressing the needs of marginalized population and has served on the boards of Shanti, The Neighborhood Youth Association, and PATH (People Assisting the Homeless).

Rebecca is grateful that her journey to recovery has finally brought her to a place where she can be a public advocate for other victims of sexual trauma, and can do so without shame. She has been a speaker at the New York State Office of Mental Health Grand Rounds at Rockland Psychiatric Center and at the Mid-Hudson Forensic Psychiatric Center affiliated with Columbia University.